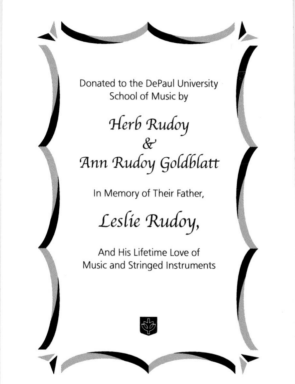

VIOLINISTS OF TO-DAY

BY THE SAME AUTHOR:

CONDUCTORS' GALLERY
(Biographical sketches of orchestral conductors)

COMPOSERS' GALLERY
(Biographical sketches of contemporary composers)

MASTERS OF THE KEYBOARD
(Great virtuosi: past and present)

FIVE GREAT FRENCH COMPOSERS
(Berlioz · César Franck · Saint-Saëns · Debussy · Ravel)

SIX GREAT RUSSIAN COMPOSERS
*(Glinka · Borodin · Mussorgsky · Tchaikovsky
Rimsky-Korsakov · Scriabin)*

COMPANION TO OPERA
(The great operas and their history)

THE ROMANCE OF THE ENGLISH THEATRE
(The story of the English stage)

JASCHA HEIFETZ

VIOLINISTS
of To-day

by
DONALD BROOK

THE MACMILLAN COMPANY
NEW YORK
1949

MADE AND PRINTED
IN ENGLAND
BY
RANKIN BROTHERS LTD., TRENCHARD STREET, BRISTOL, 1

CONTENTS

VII

LIST OF PLATES

XI

INTRODUCTION

T H E purpose of this volume is to provide the music-lover with a convenient collection of short biographies of some of the violinists we hear to-day. In it are portrayed "artists of fame and promise", as the proprietors of those excellent little galleries in Leicester Square would say, and it is perfectly obvious that the degree of fame enjoyed by the subjects varies enormously. A good proportion of British violinists are included because it is time we realized that this country can produce fine executants as well as brilliant composers, and there are a few very young players whose careers are likely to be interesting if they are given a fair chance.

It should be quite clear that no attempt has been made to produce a comprehensive collection, for that would be impossible without an unlimited supply of paper, and the absence of any particular artist does not mean that his or her merits have been overlooked.

Most of the information in this book I have gathered personally over a number of years and in recent interviews with the subjects concerned, but in the case of one or two foreign artists, some of whom I have been able to see for only very short periods, the facts gathered have been supplemented by their friends or other persons acquainted with their careers. In such cases, however, I have done my best to check their statements, and in this process I have consulted as many periodicals and reference books as possible, and I wish to acknowledge my indebtedness to such publications as *The Strad*, *The Musical Times*, *Musical Opinion*, *Current Biography* and David Ewen's *Living Musicians* (H. W. Wilson Company of New York), as well as certain other publications mentioned in the text.

I also wish to thank all those artists who have so kindly given up a great deal of their time in assisting me, and to one or two other people who have helped in a variety of ways, especially Miss C. M. O'Connor of Messrs. Harold Holt Ltd., Miss A. Hurst of Ibbs and Tillett Ltd., and Miss Lereculey of the same firm.

If this volume gives pleasure to music-lovers and is of some small service as a book of reference—for much of the information in it will not be found elsewhere—it will have fulfilled its purpose.

DONALD BROOK.

Autumn, 1947

PAUL BEARD

TO some, it may seem odd that a book devoted primarily to solo violinists should open with a sketch of an eminent orchestral leader. This is, of course, due to the fact that in order to avoid all questions of precedence the subjects in this collection of biographies are arranged alphabetically. But even if that were not the case, it would not be at all inappropriate to write first of all about Paul Beard because he holds a peculiar place in English music: a key position, as it were, of special significance. He has done quite a substantial amount of solo work in his time, but it is more as England's No. 1 orchestral leader that he now claims our attention. He stands as representative of orchestral playing at its highest level, and of a body of hard-working musicians who are too often taken for granted by those whose sense of proportion is apt to be un-balanced by the glamour that inevitably surrounds the soloist. Moreover, that reference to hard-working musicians applies not only to the members of the BBC Symphony Orchestra but to all who comprise the symphony orchestras of this country.

He was born in Birmingham on 4 August, 1901, son of a viola player who spent the greater part of his life in orchestras and chamber music ensembles. He was brought up in a musical environment, since all the family were interested in the art, and started to learn the violin when he was but three years of age under the guidance of his father. His first public appearance was made when he was six: a great success

1

that established him as a child prodigy. A drawerful
of photographs still in his possession reveals that he was
an extremely good-looking lad, and one cannot help
wondering how many old ladies' hearts were touched
by this Eton-collared phenomenon. Actually, he was
somewhat less cherubic than he appeared, for he was
a typical English schoolboy, full of fun and mischief,
and quite as fond of cricket as of music.

He toured England as a boy violinist until 1914,
when two scholarships took him to the Royal Academy
of Music to study under Rowsby Woof. He did very
well there, since his scholarships were extended, and
wrote a violin concerto which was performed in the
Queen's Hall at one of the Academy concerts.

His student days over, he returned to his native city
and resumed solo and quartet work, doing in addition
as much teaching as his fairly frequent Continental
tours would permit. Then, in the early nineteen-
twenties, he accepted the leadership of the City of
Birmingham Orchestra, which was then conducted by
Appleby Matthews, a prominent local musician. Dr.
Adrian Boult succeeded Matthews in 1924, and Paul
Beard led for him throughout his six years' sojourn in
the midland capital. Boult was succeeded in 1930 by
Leslie Heward, and Paul Beard stayed with the orchestra
until 1932 when Sir Thomas Beecham invited him to
lead the old London Philharmonic Orchestra. He
worked under the dynamic baton of "Tommy" for
four years; then, in the autumn of 1936, succeeded the
late Arthur Catterall as leader of the BBC Symphony
Orchestra.

Paul Beard accepted a professorship at the Royal
College of Music in 1937, or thereabouts, and held that
position until the outbreak of the war, when the BBC
Symphony Orchestra was evacuated to Bristol. In 1942
Sir Henry Wood felt that the Royal Academy of
Music needed the services of a first-class leader for

ANTONIO BROSA

B.

PAUL BEARD

the training of good orchestral players, so he recommended that Paul Beard, who was then with the BBC Orchestra at Bedford and who had already been elected a Fellow of the Academy, should be offered a professorship. Although he had previously been on the staff of the rival establishment at Kensington, Beard accepted the offer, and since that time has done very valuable work in preparing young violinists for orchestral appointments. It is his ambition to establish a really sound body of young orchestral players in this country. He declares that there is truly remarkable talent among the rising generation which, if properly cultivated, will enable this country to lead the world in ensemble playing before very long.

He was the youngest leader in England to complete twenty-five years as a leader of first-class professional orchestras, for in addition to the major appointments already mentioned, he spent some years in leading such ensembles as the ill-fated National Orchestra of Wales, the Spa Orchestra at Scarborough, and the Llandudno Orchestra. His experience has been wide and varied. Apart from an enormous amount of symphonic work, he has played for opera and ballet, in trios, quartets and other chamber groups, and has not scorned even light music.

Paul (as everybody seems to call him: one rarely hears a reference to "Mr. Beard") has played under almost every conductor of importance in the world, from Toscanini downwards. What a musical education that has been! He has also met scores of contemporary composers of all nations, and been privileged to discuss their works with them.

When the BBC Symphony Orchestra visited Paris early in 1947, Paul Beard and Sir Adrian Boult were awarded the Ami de Paris (something like the freedom of the city) and like other recipients of this honour, were each presented with an etching of Notre-Dame by Robert Cami.

B

This is but one of the many honours Paul has received. Perhaps it should also be said that he has been presented to every member of the Royal Family since George V. In June 1947 he was presented to Queen Wilhelmina when the BBC Symphony Orchestra visited Holland.

He is such a rich personality that it is not surprising to find that his interests are extremely varied. Consider his recreations: golf, tennis, cricket, swimming, shooting, fishing, rowing, gardening, billiards, snooker, poker . . . there seems to be no end to the list. He can talk about them, especially cricket and football, for hours on end. But even that is not the sum of his interests: he is very fond of the theatre and can discuss a play like any critic, and if you happen to catch him with a book it will probably be something by John Galsworthy, Richard Aldington, Neil Bell, Somerset Maugham, Aldous Huxley or Bernard Shaw. For sheer relaxation he favours a thriller of the better type, but it must be well constructed and logical.

Relaxation is a subject upon which he holds strong views. He feels it is absolutely essential that a musician should be able to get away from music completely at times, otherwise he cannot hope to keep up to the high standard of physical fitness that his work demands. Few people realize the strain placed upon orchestral players when they are giving half-a-dozen or more concerts a week with two or three rehearsals for each of them. The life of the musician is not an easy one, and he feels that this should be made plain to students before they make up their minds to enter the profession.

A really gifted student should be able to make excellent progress by doing no more than four hours' hard practising a day. If he tries to do more it will probably avail him nothing, since it is useless to practise when one is jaded: it can even do no small amount of harm. Paul recommends two hours in the morning and two in the evening, each session to be divided by an hour's complete break. If this plan is followed, the afternoon should be regarded as a time for relaxation of some sort—anything unconnected with music. It is only by planning one's time on lines such as these that one can be sure of approaching music with a fresh, clear mind. That is absolutely essential to healthy artistic development: Paul has seen plenty of promising young talent utterly ruined through lack of respite for the mind.

He is quite confident about the future of music in this country: his experience has taught him that if good music is well played there will always be plenty of people ready to appreciate it. This, he says, was proved once again by the 1947 Promenade season, and now that three orchestras share the work of it and are allowed sufficient time for rehearsal, he believes that this splendid institution will go from strength to strength and become a wonderful memorial to its beloved founder.

It will be noted that, unlike certain supercilious people in the musical profession, he does not speak of the Proms in a patronising and slightly contemptuous tone. The misplaced enthusiasm of some of the "Prommers" is easily understood when one considers the number of very young people in the audience who are still learning to enjoy good music. And who ever stops learning? Possibly some of the precious people who speak cynically of the Proms.

Why is it that Paul Beard does not do more solo work? The answer refutes Sir Thomas Beecham's famous remark that all orchestral players are disappointed soloists. He actually prefers leading the BBC Symphony Orchestra to travelling as a virtuoso. When he was a youth he was given the chance of deciding which type of work he would prefer, and he deliberately chose orchestral work, chiefly because of the richer experience it affords, of the comradeship that one enjoys in a good orchestra, and of the importance of the job generally. Is it so very surprising that he should prefer to play the vast repertoire of the BBC Symphony Orchestra, under the finest conductors in the world and in the company of all his friends, rather than spend a lonely life dragging a repertoire of a few dozen pieces around the world and living almost entirely in the impersonal atmosphere of hotels?

Paul loves the "family life" of the orchestra, as he calls it. There is always plenty of company, always someone with whom one can swop a story, always someone willing to come for a pint of bitter . . . always someone to share a jolly good grouse: that time-honoured privilege of the Englishman which is about all that is left to him to-day. But that is not all: he loves extending a helping hand to some passionately sincere youngster with a little more than the average skill. After all, there is always the possibility that some nervous youth just appointed to the back desk might blossom forth as the Heifetz of to-morrow. Watch Paul at a rehearsal of his section when some difficult new work has to be studied: he will gather even the most junior members around him and give them the benefit of his years of experience without making them feel like schoolchildren.

His sincerity is all the more striking when one recalls the number of bored faces one so often sees in the ranks of professional orchestras. "If music doesn't mean anything to you emotionally," he declares, "then leave it alone." Technique is not everything, for the ability to play music is not the sole qualification of a musician. Emotional satisfaction must come first.

Paul Beard is not interested in any eccentric notions about violin-playing. It is true that he generally uses only three fingers on the bow, but that is due entirely to the fact that the little finger of his right hand is unusually short, and therefore of little use. He attaches great importance to freedom of movement and graceful bowing, and considers that the motion of good *spiccato* bowing is the basis of all movements. He thinks that it is probably because the left hand needs so much training that the right is frequently neglected. "When anything goes wrong at a public performance it is usually the bow," he declares.

He was married in 1925 to Joyce Cass-Smith, a member of a well-known North of England family. They have two children: Pauline, aged seventeen, who is studying classical languages, and David, aged fifteen, who is already an able violinist and hopes to follow his father's footsteps. Their home is at Wembley Park: a very pleasant house standing in about an acre of garden which, Paul insists, he tends himself. How he finds time to keep those pleasant lawns and extensive flower beds so trim is a mystery, but when you have spent a few hours talking to this vivid personality—and he is a great conversationalist—you begin to realize that his energy knows no bounds.

ANTONIO BROSA

ALTHOUGH he is now well-known on both sides of the Atlantic as a solo violinist of great technical ability, it is perhaps in the realm of chamber music that Antonio Brosa has achieved the greatest distinction. The string quartet that for well over a decade bore his name was one of the few really first-class ensembles we possessed, and there were many expressions of regret when pressure of solo work forced him to disband it.

He was born in Spain, at Tarragona, in 1894, and was initiated into the technicalities of music at a very early age by his father, a bandmaster, who was an exceptionally fine trumpet player. For some reason, wind instruments did not make a very strong appeal to Antonio as a boy, though he loved attending his father's rehearsals: he "fell" for the fiddle and would walk about manipulating two sticks in imitation of a violinist he greatly admired. When he was five, a friend of the family gave him a half-sized fiddle, and he practised on it with such zest that within eighteen months he was allowed to play a piece in public with a discreet accompaniment by his father's band. His father rewarded him by a generous addition to that week's pocket-money, and he was very proud indeed of having earned his first "fee" so early in life.

The bandmaster was not at all keen for his son to become a musician, but the lad did so well with his little fiddle during the next few years that it would have been a pity to discourage him. When he was ten years old he was taken to Barcelona to play before Mathieu Crickboom, but as that eminent teacher was just about to return to Belgium it was arranged that the boy should study with Crickboom's colleague, Enrique Ainaud. It was at about this time that he made his first important public appearance. Ainaud was so pleased with him that he offered to train him at half-fees. The offer was gladly accepted, for the move to Barcelona meant that Brosa's father had been obliged to give up an unusually good appointment. At the end of the first month, however, Ainaud declared that he would willingly give the lessons without payment of any kind.

Brosa's playing soon aroused a great deal of interest, and after a splendid concert given at the age of fourteen he was told that the Province of Barcelona had awarded him an official grant so that he could go to Belgium to study with Crickboom. Actually, he had already visited Belgium for lessons with this master, but the grant made it possible to go again for a much longer course. Strictly speaking, he was not really entitled to the grant at all because he was not a native of Barcelona, but all conditions concerning birth and residence in the province were waived because it was felt that he possessed quite remarkable talent.

It is curious to note that during the first twenty-five years of his life, Brosa was dogged by misfortune: he met with a series of accidents that might easily have ended his career as a musician. The worst of them was when he was involved in a motor accident and fractured his left arm. He was unaware of the injury until the last item of a recital he gave immediately afterwards. In this he had to make an unusual stretch with his left hand, and as he did so he was conscious of a sharp pain near his elbow. Fortunately, after a period of convalescence, he recovered full use of the arm. On another occasion he was walking along a street in Barcelona when a balcony crashed down on the pavement only a few yards in front of him. It was this that made him wonder whether or not he was ill-fated, and one cannot blame him for making a supreme effort to get away from Barcelona once and for all!

His progress in Brussels brought him the offer of an attractive series of engagements for the autumn of 1914, but luck was still against him, for the outbreak of war in August of that year compelled him to flee to England. He arrived in London with twenty-five francs, and knew not a soul. It was a bewildering experience, and he began to wonder whether he would have to play in the streets. Fortunately, he received the assistance of an organization that was trying to help refugee musicians, and in due time was able to get sufficient work to support himself. He has always been deeply grateful for the help given to him by Edith Lyttelton, especially because it was through her that he met his wife, Margaret Dallas, an artist and a granddaughter of Sir Charles Santley, the famous singer.

For a while, Brosa accepted various orchestral jobs in order to pay his way, and his real début in this country was not made until 1919, when he gave a recital that drew a considerable amount of attention to his outstanding ability.

His famous string quartet was founded in 1925 and rose to fame quickly. A great encouragement to them was the invitation they received from the Elizabeth Sprague Coolidge Foundation to visit America, of which the outcome was that they toured the United States in 1931, 1932 and 1934. During the following four or five years they toured all over the world, but during that time Brosa's reputation as a soloist was advancing rapidly, and by 1939 he was so inundated with demands for his solo services that he was obliged to disband the quartet. Moreover, he had always been interested in solo work and sensed a disadvantage in becoming too well known as leader of the Brosa Quartet, for it is unfortunately true that in music anybody who specializes in one particular form of activity is apt to be looked upon as one who cannot, or does not wish to, do anything else. In America, for instance, he was regarded exclusively as a chamber music player until the spring of 1940. It was on 28 March of that year that he made his début as a solo violinist with the New York Philharmonic Symphony Orchestra, when he played Benjamin Britten's concerto. This concerto, as the reader is probably well aware, is a work of extreme difficulty, and the ease with which Brosa played it caused a minor sensation among many violinists who were present. It is perhaps worthy of record that while Britten was writing this work he frequently called in Brosa to act as consulting specialist, a fact that drew from Mr. William McNaught, the editor of the *Musical Times*, the remark that the composer had evidently been engaged in a search for the limit of the possible! However, Brosa's success with this concerto brought him a gratifyingly large number of offers of further engagements.

Despite his decision to concentrate upon solo work, Brosa led the Pro Arte String Quartet in America for four years during the early part of the Second World War, though this was, of course, combined with many solo appearances in the United States.

In recent years he has given several recitals in England, and many will recall his excellent broadcasts on the Third Programme, in which he has been featured prominently as a soloist. His recital at the Wigmore Hall on 15 July, 1946, gave us a splendid opportunity of admiring his wonderful technique, though there were some criticisms of his style in certain works. In the Stravinsky *Duo Concertante* he swept through the many technical difficulties as if they had been second-year exercises, and with an ease that compelled admiration. He also gave a very fine rendering of the Max Bruch Concerto No. 1.

Brosa's style is clean and neat, his intonation is invariably accurate, and his bowing is quite masterly. To almost every type of modern work it seems well suited, but it is not quite so effective in music of the eighteenth century. His interpretations of the works of contemporary composers are always conscientious and sympathetic.

He has not made many recordings in this country in recent years, the only well-known one being the Mendelssohn Concerto, for H.M.V.

Brosa has always taken the keenest interest in the works of modern English composers—he played a great deal of music by Elgar, Vaughan Williams, Bax and Frank Bridge in Germany before the war, for instance—and of his younger contemporaries he feels that Britten, Berkeley, Rubbra and Tippett, especially, are worthy of attention. He also watches carefully the work of the few Spanish composers that are now trying to make themselves heard, and has had a concerto written expressly for him by Robert Gerhard.

When discussing the subject of interpretation with him, one finds that Brosa places great emphasis upon the necessity of understanding the "language" of each composer. Music played without this understanding is like poetry read in a foreign language by someone who is entirely ignorant of the meaning of the words: it may sound quite all right to a casual listener, but to the serious and attentive person it is robbed of all its beauty.

Brosa uses the Vesuvius Strad dated 1727, and prefers a gut A string. He has tried the new nylon strings and believes that they have great possibilities, though he rarely uses them in public on account of their tendency to "whistle".

Although he accepts few private pupils he is fond of teaching, and has recently been appointed head of the violin department of Smith College, Northampton, Mass., with the title of "Artist in residence". His duties include not only teaching but the giving of regular recitals in the college. It is perhaps of interest to note that when advising young players he always urges them not to be afraid of playing in their own way. Too many violinists are striving to become imitation Heifetzes, and that is a great pity because they are stifling their own personalities and losing the art and satisfaction of expressing themselves. He also disapproves of the tendency to worship technique above everything else: the musical world seems to be full of technicians but true artists are becoming like currants in the proverbial bun. The value of playing chamber music as a means of deepening one's interpretative powers cannot be over-rated: it is an essential factor in the training of a good solo artist.

Few of his admirers are aware that Brosa is quite an accomplished painter in oils and delights in sketching. He can also speak no fewer than five languages and is now engaged in learning a sixth: Russian. His literary taste is chiefly for good fiction.

Sport of all types has always appealed strongly to him, and it does not require any very strong temptation to make him attend a football match. At one time he was also a splendid tennis player, but he confesses that in recent years his racquet has fallen into disuse. Table-tennis and billiards often occupy spare moments indoors.

IN the period between the two world wars, Adolf Busch succeeded in building up such a fine reputation as a classical violinist that to-day his name is known and respected in every country of the world, and it is worth remembering that he won his laurels, not only as a soloist whose technique could dazzle the general musical public, but also as a chamber musician whose profound artistry could impress the more discriminating type of listener.

He was born on 8 August 1891 in the Westphalian town of Siegen, son of a cabinet-maker who had for years cherished an ambition to make a name as a professional musician but who had unfortunately been kept to his trade by financial difficulties. However, this good craftsman consoled himself by making and playing violins and running an amateur orchestra, and it was a great joy to him that his small son should take such a keen interest in his hobby. When the lad was but three years of age he was given a fiddle, and it was chiefly his overwhelming desire to play in his father's little orchestra that made him practise so assiduously. The keen sense of music that he had inherited made progress very rapid, and he had already appeared in public by the time he reached his sixth birthday.

He was about ten years old when his father decided that he should have a proper musical education. As a first move in that direction he was sent to an uncle in Duisburg so that he could have the advantage of tuition from the more competent teachers in that city, but he had not been there a year when the State Director of Music recognized his great talent and secured his admission to the Musikalische Hochschule at Cologne. Here he studied under Willi Hess and Fritz Steinbach, and, a little later, became a pupil of Bram Eldering. It is interesting to note that during his student days he distinguished himself not only as a violinist but as a composer: he was barely fourteen when he had a complete symphony to his credit.

His elder brother Fritz, who was later to establish himself as a conductor, was also studying music at the time, and the strain upon the cabinet-maker's slender resources became so great that the two brothers had to accept engagements to play dance music in order to pay their way.

Concluding his course at the age of eighteen, Adolf Busch had the honour of performing his own Serenade for Orchestra at a concert arranged by his college. His playing on this occasion was particularly brilliant, and immediately afterwards he began to receive offers of engagements as a soloist in Berlin and Vienna.

His next move was to Bonn, where he took a short course of lessons with Hugo Grüters, and, incidentally, fell in love with that professor's daughter, Frieda. They married a few years later—in 1913.

His successes in Central Europe now led to his first visit to England, and he made his début in London in the spring of 1912. The critics agreed that he was one of the most promising young violinists they had heard for many a year. Some idea of their enthusiasm may be gained from *The Strad*, whose critic declared in the April issue of that year:

"He is a violinist of remarkable calibre and will, I think, shortly be in the first flight. The playing is uncompromisingly classical, but the high aims of the young artist, one feels, are by no means beyond his reach."

Commenting on Busch's playing of the Brahms Concerto the same critic said that although he had not the polish of some of the other players then before the public, no one short of Kreisler could approach him for purity of style and intense beauty of phrasing.

When he was twenty-one, Busch was invited to become the leader of the Konzertverein Orchestra, Vienna, which was then being conducted by Ferdinand Loewe. For five years he held this position, and it was during this period that he formed the first string quartet to bear his name.

In 1917, when he was only twenty-six years of age, Busch was invited to succeed Henry Marteau at the Berlin Hochschule as chief professor of the violin: the post that Joachim had held some ten years previously. This entailed removal to Berlin, of course, and severance with the Vienna orchestra, but the honour was too great to refuse. In Berlin he was able to devote more time to chamber music, and two years after his arrival in the German capital he founded another string quartet. This was the Busch String Quartet that was to become famous all over the world. Its personnel was changed somewhat during the ensuing twenty years or so, and the ensemble that did the extensive tours during the nineteen-thirties consisted of Adolf Busch as leader, Gosta Andreasson (second violin), Karl Doktor (viola) and Hermann Busch, the leader's younger brother ('cellist). When the quartet visited England in the spring of 1947, Adolf Busch's three associates were Ernst Drucker (second violin), Hugo Gottesmann (viola) and Hermann Busch.

The many fine recordings made by this quartet for H.M.V. include five Beethoven quartets: No. 11 in F minor, No. 16 in F, No. 14 in C-sharp minor, No. 15 in A minor and No. 18 in F; the Schubert Quartet in D minor; and, with Reginald Kell playing the clarinet, the Brahms Quintet in B minor, Opus 115.

Only those who have played in string quartets can

properly appreciate the tremendous amount of work that these four musicians did to bring their little ensemble to such a high standard of excellence. It has been said that they rehearsed nine hours a day for many weeks prior to some of their great achievements. The extensive tour of America that was made in 1939, for instance, opened with a series of five concerts in New York before one of the most critical audiences ever assembled in that city, and a few unfavourable or indifferent reports in the papers might have adversely affected the entire tour.

The quartet is now far-famed for its scholarly readings, impeccable style and the infinite variety of tone that all four seem to be able to produce with such ease. One feels that they never play to "make an impression": they seem quite lost in the beauty of their work.

To return to the purely biographical aspect of this sketch: it should be recorded that Adolph Busch's first visit to America was in 1931 when he made his début as a soloist in the Beethoven Concerto with the New York Philharmonic Symphony Orchestra. His playing made a deep impression upon Toscanini, and later in the same year he made a prolonged tour with the great conductor. In due course a cordial friendship sprang up between them.

The rise of Hitler to power in Germany was a matter of great concern to Busch, and although he possessed no Semitic blood himself, he protested strongly when the Nazis began their persecution of the Jews. Then came the official interference in German art, the banning of music by Jewish composers, and all the other absurdities and injustices that characterized the National Socialist regime; so he cancelled all his engagements and came to England. Later, he moved to Switzerland, and in 1935 took Swiss nationality. He then declared that he would never again play in any country that was not ruled by a free, democratic government.

Busch's name was now becoming associated with that of his talented son-in-law, Rudolf Serkin, the pianist, for they had been giving some excellent recitals together. Perhaps the most important of these took place during the 1937-8 season, when they played all the violin sonatas of Beethoven in New York. In its report, the *New York Times* declared that the highest ideals of ensemble playing had been realized. Among their recordings will be found the Brahms Sonata in A, Opus 100, No. 2; Schumann's Sonata in A minor, Opus 105; and the Beethoven "Spring" Sonata in F, Opus 24, all of which are by H.M.V.

Another of Adolf Busch's organizations is the ensemble known as the Busch Chamber Players. Their many activities have included the recording of such works as all the Bach Brandenburg Concertos for Columbia, and the same composer's Suites Nos. 1 in C, 2 in B minor, 3 in D and 4 in D, for H.M.V., as well as Mozart's Serenade in D (*Serenata notturna*, K.239). Then again there is that delightful trio in which he is associated with his younger brother and Rudolf Serkin. These three have not been heard together very often, it is true, but many music lovers will recall with pleasure their superb playing of classical trios.

Busch will long be remembered as the possessor of one of the finest bow arms in existence. His faultless phrasing one takes for granted, but his superb "elastic" *cantilena* is something that only the really great violinists seem to achieve.

His tone is somewhat harder than that of most other prominent violinists of the day: a fact that sometimes causes disappointment among those who hear him in person for the first time, particularly if they have been listening to a good deal of violin-playing reproduced by a certain type of radio set.[1] But this

[1]So many people demand radio sets that produce a woolly, "luscious" tone, irrespective of what goes into the microphone

ADOLF
BUSCH

Fox

Gramophone

MISCHA ELMAN

more metallic tone seems to suit his severely classical style, and few would wish to hear a "sensuous" tone from this reserved and somewhat austere artist. He uses the precious "Ex-Wiener Strad", dated 1732, which bears the maker's personal testimony that he made it in his eighty-ninth year. It is very brown, and heavily varnished. The tone is unusually rich and even on all four strings.

Busch has composed a variety of works for violin and piano, and has shown great understanding of the human voice in the various songs he has written. His compositions also include a good deal of chamber music and a Symphony in E, which the New York Philharmonic Orchestra performed under the direction of his brother Fritz in November 1927.

It might be recorded here that Adolf Busch received a degree of Doctor of Music at Edinburgh University during a visit to this country in 1935. At the present time he lives in New York, though one rarely finds him settled at any place for long, because he still tours extensively. Almost every musical centre of any importance in America has received visits from him, and he always likes to come to England at least once or twice every year. In 1945 he went to Reykjavik at the invitation of the Icelandic Government and gave a series of three recitals.

that manufacturers can scarcely be blamed for adjusting their wares accordingly. Unfortunately, one can scarcely hope for any improvement in the taste of the general public so long as a complete travesty of music is boomed into our cinemas.

C

ALFREDO CAMPOLI

CAMPOLI'S name was associated with light music for so many years that when he resumed classical work a few years ago his remarkable technique and deep understanding of great music came as a surprise to most of the younger members of the audiences he delighted. His older listeners, on the other hand, were more prepared for his welcome return to the concert hall, for they had many happy memories of his fine playing of the classics during the early nineteen-twenties.

Alfredo Campoli was born in Rome in 1906 and had the good fortune to enjoy a musical environment from the first. His father (who taught him his art) was a professor of the violin and leader of the St. Cecilia Conservatoire in Rome, and his mother was a prominent dramatic soprano who for several years toured with Caruso. Consequently, he was trained entirely in the Italian style. It is interesting to note that his father used to buy him gramophone records made by the eminent Italian singer Mattia Battistini (1857-1928), and always urged him to model his phrasing upon that of this fine baritone. "Listen to him and copy him upon your fiddle," his father would say. Thus, if one may use a term much abused in the world of song, Campoli acquired a "bel canto" style in his playing, and it is this that so many people admire to-day. It is said that Sir Thomas Beecham, in particular, is very enthusiastic about Campoli's style.

Campoli came to London in 1911 and made his

début as a violinist when he was very young indeed.
He has now forgotten the exact date, but he remembers
that he was giving regular public recitals when he was
but ten years of age. All manner of prizes were acquired
by him in his childhood, and soon after his twelfth
birthday he was forbidden to enter any more competitions of the festival type, for he had already won seven
first prizes, two gold medals and a silver cup!

We may now pass on to the year 1919, when he
entered the London Musical Festival and won the gold
medal for his playing of Mendelssohn's Violin Concerto.
He received the award from the hands of Princess Mary,
and when he met Her Royal Highness for a second time
some twenty years later, he was particularly gratified
to find that she still remembered their original meeting.

In the year 1921 Campoli gave a series of six recitals
at the Wigmore Hall and made a very favourable
impression upon the critics. It was as a result of this
that he was approached by the late Lionel Powell and
engaged for a series of International Celebrity subscrip-
tion concerts. So the fifteen-year-old violinist found
himself touring the British Isles with such great
personalities as Melba and Dame Clara Butt—and
enjoying it immensely.

For the next few years Campoli enjoyed a steady
run of successes, but in due course the great slump came,
and the many thousands who had flocked to hear him
became more concerned with the struggle for the
necessities of life than with attendance at violin recitals.
For the professional musician without private means, the
outlook was dark indeed. Some men left the profession
to earn their livelihoods by less precarious means, but
Campoli decided to stick to his job even if it meant
using his skill in slightly less dignified circumstances.
So he formed a small orchestra of his own and undertook broadcasting and recording of light music. This
saved the situation, and he was still able to accept

concert engagements from time to time. It should not be forgotten that even during his "light music days" Campoli played concertos in various parts of the country, including Birmingham, Bournemouth and Torquay.

When the Second World War brought a tremendous demand for the finest music, Campoli disbanded his orchestra—conscription had already begun the process, anyway—and offered his services to E.N.S.A. and C.E.M.A. Within a few weeks he was touring the country again giving concerts in military camps, factories, hospitals and so forth. Realizing that the revival of interest in music was something that had come to stay, he spent most of his leisure hours in rebuilding his extensive classical repertoire. Such concertos as the Bach E major, the Brahms, Beethoven, Bruch in G minor, Elgar, Mendelssohn, Paganini in D, Saint-Saëns No. 3 in B minor, Strauss, Tchaikovsky, Vieuxtemps No. 4 in D minor, Vivaldi and the Walton, together with two of Mozart's violin concertos (No. 4 in D and No. 6 in E-flat) and the Lalo concerto (*Symphonie Espagnole*)—all these, and dozens of violin sonatas, had to be polished and re-polished in between those seemingly endless concerts for soldiers, sailors, airmen and factory workers.

One of Campoli's earlier successes during the war years was at a Promenade concert in 1944 when, with the late Sir Henry Wood and the London Philharmonic Orchestra, he gave an outstanding performance of the Brahms Concerto. In the following year he gave a brilliant interpretation of the Tchaikovsky Concerto that drew from the critics many enthusiastic references to his dazzling technique and excellent tone. Since then he has played with the greater orchestras all over the country, frequently under the batons of such conductors as Sir Thomas Beecham, Sir Adrian Boult, Sir Malcolm Sargent and John Barbirolli, and has made several meritorious broadcasts.

For sheer technique, Campoli has few equals in this country. People who had the pleasure of hearing the Kreisler arrangement of the Paganini Concerto in D at a Promenade concert in August, 1946, will for many years remember his wizardry. Even those who normally dislike "virtuoso music" of this type admitted that they had experienced a physical thrill.

It might surprise some people to know that Campoli does not care for this sort of music personally: he dislikes these gymnastic displays of his remarkable technique. His real love is for Brahms—his favourite composer, by the way—whose Concerto means more to him than all the works of the "virtuoso composers" put together. He also adores Mozart, and to those who think that Mozart is easy to play he declares emphatically that the proper interpretation of the music of this genius demands superb artistry, and nothing less. He realizes that it is more or less his duty to give the public the sort of music they want him to play, but he wishes they would forget about this "brilliant technique" stuff for a while. He has no desire to be known as a musical magician.

Although the musical public generally have not had sufficient opportunity of appreciating it, Campoli's particular style seems admirably suited to the works of Bach: hear him play that difficult unaccompanied Chaconne, for instance, or the exacting Adagio and Fugue from the Sonata in G minor, and you will probably agree that he might well become a Bach specialist. His refined tone and perfect intonation, and the delightful way in which he can caress a plaintive theme—these qualities, together with the sparkle he can put into a vivacious movement, are those that mark the difference between a mediocre and an inspired execution of Bach's music. Incidentally, Campoli is the only violinist in England who has broadcast the Bach Chaconne four times. He is also remarkably good in the unaccompanied Partitas, of which he is extremely fond.

Of Campoli's many recordings, mention might be made of the Sonata in G minor by Tartini and the Bach-Franko *Arioso* (Decca), the Concerto No. 1 in G minor by Max Bruch and the Saint-Saëns Introduction and Rondo Capriccioso, both of which were recorded with the London Symphony Orchestra under Walter Goehr for Columbia, and the same company's recording of Paganini's *Moto Perpetuo*.

Campoli adheres to the Italian style of playing, although he regards Heifetz as the greatest living master of the strings. He uses all his fingers on the bow except in *spiccato* passages, when he finds that by lifting the fourth finger he can make the bow rebound better. He has used several fiddles during his career: for many years he preferred a Landolfi, then he changed to a J. B. Rogrius, but now he generally plays a Guadagnini. He uses metal-covered "Thomastik" strings, and prefers this Viennese make to any of the new types now being made in America. He has tried the new plastic-covered strings but dislikes them.

As far as possible, Campoli sets aside a period of each day for practice, believing in the "daily dose" principle. Then there are sessions of study during which he writes his programme notes, sometimes making use of his wonderful collection of over 2,000 gramophone records. These are played on a very fine electric reproducer that was built to his own specification.

To conclude with a few personal notes: he is an exceptionally good tennis, bridge and snooker player. For several years he played table tennis in the London League and earned the reputation of being one of the most formidable players in the metropolitan area. His reading is almost entirely of books on music, bridge and tennis.

RAYMOND COHEN

THIS book might easily become monotonous if it dealt with only the more celebrated type of artist, so let us turn to youth for a diversion and meet a talented young violinist who, unless we are very much mistaken, is destined to become one of the leading virtuosi of to-morrow. Towards the end of 1946 that eminent conductor John Barbirolli described Raymond Cohen as "the most brilliantly gifted young English violinist I have heard for many a day", and as most musicians concede, Barbirolli is a man of vision.

Manchester has given us some fine musicians, and Raymond Cohen is justly proud of having been born in that city in 1919. He had the advantage of a musical home, since both his parents were—and still are—passionately fond of music. His mother would never have met his father (a gifted amateur violinist) had music-making not brought them together. So it was not unnatural that Raymond should have taken to music at a very early age, as did his brother Cecil, who, incidentally, is now making an impression in Manchester as conductor of the orchestra run by the Adult Education Committee.

Raymond was educated at Manchester Grammar School where, at the age of eleven, he caused a sensation by playing superbly at a school concert. As he rose in the school his thoughts turned more and more towards music as a possible career, and finally, his doubts about the precariousness of it were suppressed, if not extinguished, when at the age of fifteen he won the

Brodsky Scholarship to the Royal Manchester College
of Music and in the same year was honoured with an
engagement to play in the Hallé Orchestra. Thus he
earned the distinction of being the youngest member
ever known in that orchestra since its foundation in
1858. He was probably also the youngest member of
a professional orchestra in England at that time.

At the Royal Manchester College he became a
pupil of Henry Holst, and for four years studied under
that very able violinist. He took the piano as his second
study, and it should also be recorded here that Lionel
Falkman was partly responsible for his musical education.

While he was still a student he received a gratifyingly
large number of engagements: he continued to play in
the Hallé Orchestra, and was only eighteen when he
was chosen to lead the Blackpool Orchestra. Then he
was soon to distinguish himself by taking part in chamber
music at the Manchester Tuesday Midday Concerts,
and gradually he was able to rise to local eminence
as a soloist. He claims that when he was only twenty
he had another distinction to his credit: apart from
Yehudi Menuhin he was the only violinist to have
played in this country three concertos at a single
concert. These were the Bach E major, Mendelssohn
and Brahms, which he performed with the Hallé
Orchestra on a memorable day in 1940.

War, alas! has respect for neither art nor youth,
and it was with very mixed feelings that Raymond
Cohen received his calling-up papers—it was actually
only a few weeks after that triumphant accomplishment
with the three concertos! The beauty and inspiration,
the glamour and thrill, the joy of life that can be so
rich and exciting when youth and talent and great
music all combine—all this was now overshadowed.
One does not require much of an imagination to
visualize the disruption in this young man's life; from
the beauty of music-making in a cultured environment

to the ugliness of barrack life, but Cohen took it all philosophically, and soon discovered that things have a way of sorting themselves out—that there was quite a large number of men in the army who were concerned with something else besides "pools" and "the dogs", food and women. He found himself, in due course, a member of the Royal Corps of Signals, where his musical ability was recognized, and it was not long before he was playing the clarinet in the band. The speed with which he took to this instrument was really quite remarkable, and he might have become very fond of it if he had been given more interesting music to play. There were also some amusing incidents which, even if they jarred upon his musical sensitivity, did tend to make life more colourful. There was the occasion, for instance, when at the request of his bandmaster he transformed himself from third clarinettist to solo violinist and played a battered version of the Mendelssohn Violin Concerto with military band accompaniment!

Cohen used to ponder a good deal upon army life and the strange ideas possessed by some of those with whom he had to rub shoulders, but found—as most Englishmen do sooner or later—that the cultivation of a sense of humour is the best means of preserving one's sanity in these "enlightened" times. His greatest difficulty was in finding somewhere to practise the long-suffering fiddle that accompanied him from station to station. The recreation rooms provided by the military authorities were generally reverberating with jazz, so in order to keep up his vitally-important practice, Cohen would go out into the fields or, in wet weather, take his fiddle to the bathroom, or some less uplifting place, draw forth tattered leaves of Bach, Brahms, Beethoven or Mozart, and resolutely prepare himself for a career in the wonderful post-war world that he was hearing so much about.

Such stoicism surely deserved a rich reward, and it came when, while still a soldier, he won the coveted

International Carl Flesch Award in 1945. This new competition is open to violinists of any nationality under thirty years of age, who are required to play a concerto and an unaccompanied Bach sonata. It is organised by the Guildhall School of Music, London, and the adjudicators in that particular year were Edric Cundell (the Principal of the School), Jean Pougnet, Albert Sammons and Max Rostal.

When at last he was demobilized—after six years in the army—Cohen was delighted to find that musical folk had not forgotten his early successes, and it was therefore a pleasant surprise when the difficulties of re-establishing himself proved less arduous than he had anticipated. John Barbirolli was one of the first to welcome him back—with an engagement to appear as a soloist with the Hallé Orchestra. Then again, the terms of the Carl Flesch Award made it possible for him to play the Mendelssohn Concerto with the London Philharmonic Orchestra, conducted by George Weldon, at the Stoll Theatre, London, on 5 May, 1946. Engagements to appear as a soloist with the London Symphony Orchestra, the BBC and other orchestras soon followed, and so did various opportunities to prove his worth as a chamber musician by giving sonata recitals in various parts of the country. It might be said here that his interest in chamber music is such that in order to widen his knowledge and appreciation of it he has made himself very proficient on the viola as well, though he has no intention of playing it as a solo instrument in public.

Cohen's repertoire is now quite large, and covers most of the various "schools" of music. In it we find about forty concertos and a suggestion that he is specially attracted towards the works of Brahms, Elgar, Sibelius, Bloch, Busoni, Barber, Glazounov, Prokofiev and that talented young Soviet composer Khatchaturian: an interesting list for an artist under thirty. Of our contemporary English composers it might be added that he specially admires William Walton and Benjamin Britten.

Having spoken of specialization, one should point out that Cohen does not believe in specialization if it means the exclusion of other types of music. He does not favour programmes that give too much of the work of a single composer, and definitely dislikes whole evenings of the music of any one man, for he believes in the significance of contrast, and goes so far as to hold that a true, well-balanced musician should be interested in all types of music including the so-called light music and even "swing". It is the appreciation of all combined, he declares, that makes the right sort of musician. A good instrumentalist should be able to adapt himself readily to solo, chamber, orchestral or even dance band work.

Cohen is a firm believer in the principle of listening to the great in order to become great yourself: he spends hours listening intently to the recordings of Kreisler, Heifetz, Szigeti and the late Emanuel Feuermann, and rarely misses an opportunity of hearing any of the leading violinists in person, or on the radio. He is also convinced that the violinist can learn a great deal from the singer, especially in the art of phrasing and producing a good tone. He particularly delights in the singing of Gigli, Kirsten Flagstad and Tauber. As far as sheer artistry is concerned, he associates Tauber with Kreisler. Cohen does not sing himself, but he says that if he had a voice he would know how to sing! He did a little in an Army male voice choir during the war, and that, he says, was the end of what little voice he had. He has a feeling that the Americans, especially, have an unusual ability to combine all the good qualities in singing.

His entire approach to violin-playing is based on the teaching of Carl Flesch, who was, he believes, the greatest violin teacher of all time. He is exceptionally loose-fingered, and is not absolutely bound to practise every day to keep up to concert standard: he can, for instance, go for a week's holiday and scarcely notice the lapse in practice. Like most good violinists, he believes that chamber music offers the finest training for any string-player: it is indispensable to the soloist and of the utmost help to the orchestral player, since it makes one listen to the other parts, which is the basis of all good ensemble playing. Cohen is also interested in the art of improvisation, and for that reason is an admirer of Artie Shaw! Conducting, too, appeals to him, and he feels it to be not at all unlikely that in later years he might aspire to a baton. "Nerves" do not worry him, but he says he is conscious that they are there!

Cohen's greatest difficulty at the present time is to find a suitable fiddle. Whenever he has an important public engagement he is obliged to borrow an instrument, for his own is quite inadequate. And that explains why he is so rarely in his hotel when on tour: he spends every available hour in searching music and antique shops in the hope that someday he will pick up a Strad for a few pounds! He claims to have scoured more pawn shops than any other violinist in England.

Tennis is his principal recreation, but he can also play a wicked game of snooker when he is in the mood for it. His interest in dance music has already been noted, but he never goes to dances. "Of course," he adds, "if the right sort of partner came along that would make all the difference, and then I probably should!"

MISCHA ELMAN

MANY years have passed since the recitals of Elman caused a sensation in the popular press, and now that the radio has provided good music on tap in almost every home it is doubtful whether any violinist will again be able to stir audiences of thousands to such a pitch of excitement as did this world-famous artist in the early decades of the present century. We have now become accustomed to a very high standard of playing and are less inclined to heap extravagant praise upon the heads of celebrities for superb playing of the more popular classics. Nevertheless, the name of Elman will take a prominent place in the history of violin- playing.

He was born in the Russian town of Talnoye on 20 January 1892. His father, a Jewish teacher, was an enthusiastic amateur violinist and gave him a small violin when he reached the age of four. This started him on the road to fame, for within a year he had made such a favourable impression upon the Countess Orosova that she was convinced he would become a world-famous violinist. She offered to adopt him and give him the finest musical education that money could buy, but stipulated that he should renounce his Jewish faith and become a Christian. His father, however, would not agree to this condition, and made up his mind to keep the matter of his son's education in his own hands, despite his very limited means. Great sacrifices had to be made for the boy, and Elman has always felt deeply indebted to his father, who, he declares, did far more for him than his means permitted.

At the age of twelve, Mischa Elman was admitted
to the Imperial School of Music at Odessa and became
a pupil of Alexander Fidelmann. At about the same
time his father took him to Berlin to fulfil a concert
engagement, and an incident occurred that very nearly
put an end to the lad's career altogether. They stayed
at a small hotel that was lit by gas: a great novelty in
those days, especially for one who had come from a
Russian town in which illumination was provided
almost entirely by oil lamps and candles. When he
went to bed on the night of his arrival, Mischa simply
blew out the small gas jet. If his bedroom window had
not been left open the result might have been fatal. As
it happened, he awoke in the early morning feeling
horribly sick and light-headed, and it was feared that
he would have to cancel the concert. After lunch,
however, he felt rather better, but when the time for
the concert came, he was still far from well. Determined
to fulfil his contract, he went on to the platform rather
giddily and started to play. He got through the
Tchaikovsky Concerto and played the Bach Chaconne
superbly, but just before the end of the last item on the
programme he collapsed.

In these days it is hard to realize that until Elman
got to Odessa he had never even seen a pianoforte.
When he played his first concerto he had never heard
a proper symphony orchestra! Yet when Leopold
Auer visited the Imperial School shortly after Elman's
first term he found him already an accomplished
musician, even though the lad had been so nervous
when first asked to play before this famous violinist that
he had let his bow fall to the ground.

Auer then told Elman's father that if he would
bring the lad to St. Petersburg, he would take him under
his personal supervision. This opportunity of becoming
a pupil of so famous an artist was not to be missed, but
a difficulty arose immediately owing to the authorities'
refusal to allow Elman's father to reside in the city.

Various petitions were made in vain, and finally Auer wrote to the authorities himself, saying that he would resign his position at the Conservatoire if they refused residence to the father of "the most talented pupil ever offered to me".

Elman soon became Auer's favourite pupil, and the great teacher made up his mind that the boy should appear in public at an important concert as soon as an opportunity presented itself. At about that time another brilliant violinist, Vecsey, was visiting St. Petersburg and causing quite a sensation. To the amazement of his fellow professors, Auer calmly announced one day that he had a pupil who was better than Vecsey; and a chance to satisfy their curiosity came about a month later when Auer was taken ill just before one of his most important concerts. He therefore sent the thirteen-year-old Elman to take his place, and to the astonishment of all, the lad played the Mendelssohn Concerto and Paganini's *Moto Perpetuo* almost as well as his renowned master could have done. The audience refused to leave the hall until he had played no less than half-a-dozen encores.

Elman was still only a boy when Auer arranged for him to play with the famous Colonne Orchestra during their visit to Pavlovsk. Knowing Édouard Colonne's hatred of child prodigies, Auer did not tell him Elman's age when making the arrangements, and not until the famous conductor saw young Mischa waiting to go on the platform did he realize that he had engaged a child. He was furious, and flatly refused to continue with the programme. Frantic attempts were made to assure him that Elman had the recommendation of Auer himself and was well capable of doing justice to the music, but Colonne was adamant. " I have never yet played with a child, and I refuse to start now," he retorted. So Elman had to play with piano accompaniment while conductor and orchestra sat listening. The quality of his performance may be measured by

Colonne's action as soon as he finished playing: the eminent conductor went straight up to him and said: "My friend, I apologise. Will you honour me by playing with my orchestra in Paris?" A few months later Elman scored a gigantic success with the Colonne Orchestra in the Mendelssohn Concerto.

Such were the triumphs of Elman's childhood. Much could be written of his performances before the various crowned heads of Europe, and so forth, but that would make tedious reading. The only royal personage that need be mentioned here is the Grand Duke of Mecklenburg-Strelitz, one of the Tsar's relations, who took a great interest in Elman for many years, and presented him with a valuable Amati fiddle.

Elman's English début took place at the Queen's Hall on 21 March, 1905—soon after his thirteenth birthday. The reception given to this bushy-haired, blue-eyed boy can be imagined from the report in the April issue of *The Strad*:

"This young violinist, who has already created a perfect furore on the continent, has no reason to complain of want of appreciation on the part of a critical London audience; and his first appearance in England . . . was a veritable triumph. From the moment he stepped on to the platform until he had played his last encore at 11.20 p.m. (and even then the public seemed to want some more) his success in this country was an assured thing. He tackled the terrific difficulties of Tchaikovsky's D major Concerto as though they were a mere bagatelle, and although Auer said it was almost unplayable, and Hanslick (who ought to have known better) called it all sorts of dirty names, this little fellow literally[1] 'waltzed round it', made light of its technical pitfalls, and gave a rendering of it so thoroughly in accord with the spirit in which it was written, that

[1] Not literally, one hopes.

ALFREDO
CAMPOLI

Paul Tanqueray

Gramophone

SZYMON GOLDBERG

the audience literally rose at him. . . . His playing of Beethoven's Romance in G . . . was deliciously tender and sympathetic. . . . When I left the hall the crowd was still clamouring (somewhat thoughtlessly) for another display."

Incidentally, Elman's manager had a summons served upon him for allowing a boy under the prescribed age to play in public at an evening performance without a magistrate's order, but it was afterwards withdrawn.

For the next eight or nine years, Elman spent much of his time in England, and as older music-lovers will recall, became a public favourite. With Caruso and Melba he performed before King Edward, and when His Majesty asked him what he thought of London, he replied that, best of all, he liked talking to the policemen. This was, of course, long before the subject was made the basis of a joke.

A distinguished American musician, after hearing Elman play at a charity concert at Covent Garden in December 1905, caused a sensation by declaring publicly that the boy had convinced him of the authenticity of the doctrine of reincarnation, since it was obvious to him that such playing as his could be explained only by the fact that Elman must have been a great violinist in a previous existence!

If we discount all the extravagant reports we still find that sober musical opinion was very favourably impressed. In the *Musical Times* of July 1906, we read :

"Mischa Elman, the wonderful boy violinist, whose readings are so matured that he would seem to have very little to learn, played at the Queen's Hall on 29 May and 11 June. On the latter occasion, supported by the London Symphony Orchestra, he was heard for the first time here in the Brahms Concerto in D, interpreting the solo part with astonishing depth of expression and technical mastery."

D

There can be no doubt that his technical displays were quite extraordinary for a lad of his age: his spring bowing, double stoppings, *pizzicatos* and flying *staccatos* were most fascinating to anybody with even a slight knowledge of violin playing, and he always drew a delightfully warm tone from his Amati that was most pleasing to the ear.

Oscar Hammerstein persuaded Elman to make his first visit to America towards the end of 1908, and it was proposed that for his début in New York he should give a two-hour programme accompanied by the Russian Symphony Orchestra. The management on the other side of the Atlantic took exception to this, however, and declared that no American audience would tolerate two hours of "unadulterated violin-playing". They acquiesced eventually, however, and in due course discovered that the audience concerned not only "tolerated" the performance but demanded no less than twenty-two more. Reporting the initial concert, the *Tribune* said:

"Elman's tone is large and full. His notes were produced with a precise faith to the pitch that was comforting to hear. . . . In the double stopping, his octaves, and especially the rapid passages, the violinist reached a lofty standard of proficiency, while his cantilena was admirable, full and sustained."

Elman made his home in England until the outbreak of the Great War in August, 1914. By that time so many thousands of "Elmanites" would flock to his recitals that only the Albert Hall could cope with the demand for seats. His presence had also been demanded at Buckingham Palace on several occasions, for it was well known that Queen Alexandra was especially fond of his playing.

It is perhaps worth recording that Tsar Nicholas II issued a special order exempting Mischa Elman from any form of military service on account of his great

value as an artist. Elman received a personal letter
from the Tsar which begged him to keep out of all
danger because "Russia would not wish harm to come
to one of her great geniuses."

In America, Elman's fame increased year by year,
and in 1923 he became a citizen of the United States.
He married an American woman, Helen Katten, two
years later. His wife's wedding gift to him was the
superb Madame Recamier Strad, reputed to be worth
at least £10,000. It is dated 1717.[1]

Chamber music had always appealed strongly to
this distinguished violinist, although during the first
twenty years of his career he took little part in it
publicly. The Elman Quartet was not founded until
1924, but then he proved his ability in this sphere of
musical activity by subduing his outstanding personality
in a manner that would have done credit even to a
veteran player: he never outshone his partners as so
often happens when a soloist leads a quartet. According
to one critic, the performance of the Mozart B-flat
Quartet at their first concert was "positively thrilling".
Their recording of part of the Beethoven *Emperor*
Quartet, together with the familiar Andante Cantabile
from Tchaikovsky's Quartet Opus 11 (H.M.V.) are still
"best sellers" in this country.

Well over two million of Elman's gramophone
records have been sold, and the favourites in this country
are light solos such as the Wieniawski *Légende*, Opus 17,
Massenet's *Thaïs* Meditation, Tchaikovsky's *Mélodie*,
Opus 42 No. 3, and that ever-popular excerpt *Le Cygne*
(Saint-Saëns), all of which are H.M.V.

It would be very wrong, nevertheless, to conclude
from this that Elman's repertoire consists principally of
the more popular classics. It includes an imposing
range of the finest compositions for the violin, and his
interest in contemporary music was recognized recently

[1]Elman is also the owner of the Joachim Strad.

by the Czech composer Bohuslav Martinu, who dedicated a new concerto to him. Elman gave the first performance of this at the Carnegie Hall, New York, with the Boston Symphony Orchestra directed by Koussevitzky in January 1944. His masterly interpretation of this difficult work was acclaimed enthusiastically by the critics, and he afterwards made a recording of it. Another outstanding performance of this work was given by him at the Berkshire (U.S.A.) Musical Festival in the summer of 1946.

Elman's concerts in America now seem to have become something of a national institution, and reports of them, such as the one he gave in 1946 when he played the Bruch Concerto No. 1 at the Lewisohn Stadium, suggest that he has lost none of his amazing technical precision. His Carnegie Hall concert in the same year created a furore.

The outstanding feature of his playing is not the technical mastery of his instrument, however, nor yet the satisfying breadth of tone, but that spiritual Hebraic quality that artists of Jewish ancestry seem to be able to put into music of a sombre mood. He has, on the other hand, a gift for boisterous *vivace* which, combined with an ability to make a really remarkable technical display, can prove quite irresistible. There is still a certain amount of Russian temperament in his style.

Elman's home in New York is a favourite rendezvous for his friends, for his "musical evenings" are a great delight to those who have the privilege of joining him for a trio or quartet. Good music and lively conversation are enjoyed in turn, and everything invariably centres around the subject of this sketch: a short and rather stocky figure, round-faced and short-sighted. He has a tremendous sense of humour, and is more tolerant and kindly than many of the fashionable musicians in America to-day. Hear him talking about jazz, for instance, and you will find that he is not at all alarmed by its effect upon the rising generation. He believes it is useless to protest against it, for it is the natural expression of the youth of to-day, and provides an outlet for their energy. Some of it is very bad music, of course, but there is much that has a certain merit of its own, and the opportunities it affords for improvisation are by no means inconsiderable. Elman feels that "swing" is bound to exert a strong influence upon serious music of the future, in fact we can already see the effect of it in the work of many of our younger composers.

On the subject of musical criticism, Elman is often outspoken because he feels that one can over-develop the critical faculty to such an extent that one loses the ability to enjoy music. The critic who concentrates upon observing every little fault in a performance never enjoys it, in fact he is so engrossed in detail that he does not really hear the work as a whole. Music can bring pleasure and satisfaction to the emotions even when there are faults that offend the intellect.

As these opinions suggest, Elman is an unusually placid musician; the very antithesis of the petty, "temperamental" virtuoso. He does not fly into rages, nor does he tear at what remains of his hair whenever some trifle annoys him. Those who have had the honour of accompanying him on the piano agree that it is easier to work with him than almost any other famous executant in America to-day.

Finally, Elman still takes an interest in the welfare of his native land, although he has grown to love America and all that it stands for. When the Russians began the restoration of the Tchaikovsky Museum at Klin he sent them a complete set of his recordings of the great Russian composer's music. He hopes that the day is not far off when America, Soviet Russia and Britain will work together in perfect concord, and that there will then be a free exchange of ideas between the artists of all countries.

SZYMON GOLDBERG

A YOUNG violinist of international reputation, who has in recent years made a very favourable impression both in Britain and America, is Szymon Goldberg: a sensitive artist equipped with excellent technique and a real understanding of the classics. The series of recitals he gave in the Third Programme during the late autumn of 1947, in which he played the six unaccompanied violin sonatas of Bach, gave the more discriminating listener ample evidence of his ability.

He is of Polish origin, having been born at Wloclawek, near Warsaw, in 1909, son of a mill-owner. He was one of five brothers, all of whom became fairly proficient on some sort of musical instrument, so there was plenty of music-making in the home to stimulate his innate love of the art.

When he was very small, Szymon Goldberg was given a mandoline, and he displayed his *flair* for music on this instrument with such enthusiasm that his parents lost no time in buying him a violin which, they decided, would provide him with greater opportunities to develop his skill. At the age of seven he was sent to a local teacher, and within a year had progressed sufficiently to be accepted for training by Czaplinski, an able teacher who was a pupil of the eminent Ottokar Sevčik. It was Czaplinski who turned the lad into a sound musician and made his parents realize that he had immediate possibilities in the concert hall. So Szymon was sent to Warsaw to study with Michalowicz, a teacher with a reputation for the grooming of infant prodigies, and at the age of nine, he made his début.

Fortunately, Szymon's parents did not allow his gifts to be exploited at the expense of his musical education, and instead of permitting him to be taken about the country to earn money by charming old ladies with pretty little solos they sent him to Berlin to study with Carl Flesch, and for the next seven years he worked with this world-famous violinist and (during the master's absences) with his assistant, Richard Harpzer.

When he was twelve he played the Paganini D major Concerto and the Bach E major at a most successful public concert, and within two years had the honour of appearing as soloist with the Berlin Philharmonic Orchestra, with whom he played the same two works and one of the Joachim concertos in a single programme. This memorable concert firmly established him as a virtuoso, and he began to receive offers of engagements from all parts of Europe. Most of the travelling he did during the next two years, however, was in Germany.

At sixteen he was offered the leadership of the Dresden Philharmonic Orchestra, and realizing what a splendid opportunity this was to any musician with still a lot to learn, he accepted it, and for the next four years led that fine ensemble under many of the world's greatest guest conductors.

Goldberg was barely twenty when he was invited to accept the leadership of the Berlin Philharmonic Orchestra, which in those days was considered by many critics to be the finest orchestra in the world. At first he was co-leader with Henry Holst, but after a while assumed sole responsibility, and for a further period of four years held this important post under Dr. Furtwängler.

During his years as an orchestral leader, Goldberg gave many notable solo performances in most of the larger musical centres of Europe, and was associated with Hindemith and Feuermann in a remarkably fine trio. Many connoisseurs of chamber music will recall their visits to England, when they recorded for Columbia.

Goldberg's first visit to America was in 1938, when he made his début at Carnegie Hall. A tour of the United States was planned during the early years of the Second World War, but unfortunately he was in Java when the Japanese arrived, and was taken prisoner, so the projected tour did not materialise.

He and his wife were interned in Java for two-and-a-half years; an experience that he is not likely to forget. The story of his arrest is rather interesting because, apart from the personal angle, it concerns the rescue of his precious Stradivarius (the "Liegnitz", dated 1711, which was originally the property of a Silesian nobleman). The Japanese military police came for them one night, gave them scarcely time to dress, and after taking them away for the usual interrogation, proceeded to seal up the house in which they had been living. A friendly neighbour watched this process with interest and observed that one small window had escaped the attention of the soldiers. At great personal risk he climbed in through this window, found the Strad (which had not attracted the attention of the police, probably because of its well-worn case) and threw it over a nearby fence into the garden of the doctor who lived next door. That was all he dared to do. Fortunately the doctor was a keen amateur violinist, and on finding so valuable a fiddle in his garden guessed that it had been deposited there by someone who was anxious that it should not fall into the hands of the Japanese. So the kindly physician put it into a place of safety and eventually had the pleasure of returning it to its grateful owner. Goldberg's various bows, and the whole of his music library, were never recovered.

During those weary years of internment Szymon Goldberg played a great deal of music entirely from memory for the pleasure of his fellow internees. He will always remember the incredible ignorance and suspicion shown by the Japanese whenever he was interviewed by them. They had absorbed even the silliest absurdities of the Nazi propaganda with a child-like faith in its accuracy, and repeatedly demanded of him his number in the international Jewish underground movement of which they were certain he was a member!

Soon after his release he received from Singapore a cable sent by Erik Chisholm, who was organising musical activities for ENSA in that great sea-port, inviting him to appear there as a soloist with an orchestra that had been assembled to give concerts to Service personnel. This gave him a welcome opportunity to resume his profession, and for two months he visited camps of soldiers, sailors and airmen, playing varied programmes consisting chiefly of the more popular classics.

Then followed a four-months' tour of Australia, after which he returned to Europe and spent much of his time in Great Britain. As this book goes to press he is planning another extensive tour of the United States.

Although he has made a considerable reputation in the classics as a recitalist, concerto-soloist and chamber musician, Goldberg has also won the esteem of many contemporary composers for his sympathetic interpretation of their works. He particularly admires Hindemith, not merely because of his friendship with that composer, but because of the rich variety and true originality that is to be found in his compositions.

He uses American strings: aluminium-covered A and D, silver-covered G, and the usual steel E. The only nylon strings he has tried up to the time of writing have not impressed him very favourably, but he is interested in the experiments that are being made with them.

Szymon Goldberg was married in 1931 to Anna Maria Manasse, who for some years was known as a mezzo-soprano in chamber opera—chiefly in Germany. She was trained by Madame Schnabel (wife of Artur Schnabel, the eminent pianist) but rarely sings in public nowadays, for much of her time is now taken up with sculpture.

FREDERICK GRINKE

TO the jaded playing that one so often hears nowadays, the art of Frederick Grinke forms a perfect contrast. Here is a young violinist of undoubted skill who puts every ounce of his enthusiasm into the work he loves. It is obvious to anyone who watches him closely on the platform that he enjoys every minute of his playing: he seems to perform as much for his own satisfaction as for the pleasure of his audience.

He was born in Winnipeg, Canada, on 8 August, 1911, and started learning to play the violin when he was about nine years of age, his master being John Waterhouse, a well-known Canadian teacher. An unusually sharp and adaptable lad, he made rapid progress and was soon playing in public. He could not have been more than eleven or twelve when he made his first broadcast, and this was soon followed by more public engagements, especially when at the age of fifteen he formed a trio.

It should be emphasized, however, that those early years were not without their difficulties. Money had to be found to buy a violin suitable for public performances, to pay his teacher, to furnish him with an ever-growing library and so forth, but this ambitious boy was not easily deterred: to supplement his musical earnings he obtained a part-time job with a local tradesman, whom he assisted after school hours, and made himself financially independent.

He continued to study and win prizes in local competitions until, at the age of sixteen, he won not only

45

the Matthew Scholarship for Manitoba but the Associated Board Scholarship for the whole of Canada, which enabled him to come to London to study at the Royal Academy of Music. He became a pupil of Rowsby Woof, and soon began taking almost every prize for solo and chamber music playing that came his way. Sir Henry Wood was of course quick to observe the promise in this vivacious youth, and chose him to lead the Royal Academy Orchestra when he was only in his second year.

Grinke was still a student at the Academy when he became the second violinist in the Kutcher String Quartet, with whom he was associated for over six years and gained experience of the greatest value. He also formed a piano trio with two fellow-students, Florence Hooton and Dorothy Manley. In later years Kendall Taylor replaced Miss Manley, and although the trio has now been disbanded, Grinke and Taylor do a great deal of sonata-playing in public.

When he was twenty-one, Grinke went to Switzerland for a whole summer and studied with Adolph Busch at the latter's beautiful house outside Basle. He has many happy memories of that delightful course; of looking down upon the gaily-illuminated city at night from the lovely gardens of Busch's house; of long walks amidst inspiring scenery and swimming in the open-air pool. Busch always used to stress the importance of keeping fit in order to stand the strain of a musical career.

A few years later he went for further lessons to Carl Flesch, both in London and at Spa, Belgium. Students from all over the world made up the classes of this master: some came to play, others to listen and gain experience from the mistakes of their fellows. Many violinists who have since risen to fame were to be found there: Ginette Neveu, for instance, and Ida Haendel. Grinke will never forget how nervous he felt at those classes. He was then receiving important public engagements—he was to play that very season at a

Promenade concert—but nothing was so great an ordeal as playing to Carl Flesch before such a critical audience.

Grinke was still only twenty-one when he was approached by Sir Hamilton Harty, who had just been appointed conductor of the London Symphony Orchestra, and asked if he would accept the leadership of that body if it were offered to him. He had always longed to lead a full symphony orchestra and was very excited at this enquiry, but the directors eventually decided that he was too young for such a responsible position, and the offer was never made. A few years later he received invitations to lead several other leading symphony orchestras, but as he was then well on the way to establishing himself as a solo artist he refused them all. The one leadership he did accept, however, was that of the Boyd Neel Orchestra; that small but highly-trained string orchestra which has established an enviable reputation for itself not only in this country but in many of the larger musical centres of Europe. His first appearance with them was at the Salzburg Festival in 1937, when they gave the first performance of the *Variations on a Theme of Frank Bridge* by Benjamin Britten. He always enjoyed playing with this orchestra because, being small, it allowed more opportunity for individual effort: it was more like a chamber ensemble. With them he toured all over Austria, Holland, Portugal, Australia and New Zealand, and he has recently resigned only because he wishes to concentrate entirely upon solo work.

Frederick Grinke is now a professor of the Royal Academy of Music, and has had the honour of being elected a Fellow. He has no eccentric notions about teaching, but feels very strongly that one should not play the violin unless one really enjoys doing so: an audience can always tell whether an artist is playing because he really loves his art or merely because he wants his fee. Another point is that he firmly believes in every pupil developing his own individuality, and not slavishly imitating any particular "ideal". "No pupil should be an exact copy of his master," he declares, "otherwise the art would make little progress."

In 1940 Grinke volunteered for the Royal Air Force and became a member of the R.A.F. Symphony Orchestra, which was conducted by Wing Commander O'Donnell and had in its ranks many of Britain's leading musicians. With them he travelled many thousands of miles, particularly during their visit to America, when he frequently appeared as a soloist. On that tour he often had to practise on the train, generally in a small compartment at the end of the corridor in which the orchestra's instruments were kept. Anybody who has travelled extensively in America will know what that means! He once had to prepare a difficult work while the train was speeding across the plains of Texas and through the Rocky Mountains. It was swaying from side to side and every few moments would lurch violently, so that Grinke, who was balanced with one foot in the corridor and the other among the instrument-cases, was kept in a state of constant anxiety lest his precious instrument, or its bow, should be damaged. He also collected a record number of bruises on that tour, which ended very dramatically for him, since he was flown across the Atlantic for the sole purpose of playing the Bax concerto at the Albert Hall. There was something rather thrilling about swooping nearly half-way across the world—in wartime, too—solely because he was wanted in London to play a single work.

Another outstanding recollection of his service with the R.A.F. Orchestra is of the occasion when they were flown to Potsdam for the Three-Power Conference. The string section played at a dinner given by Mr. Churchill in honour of Stalin and President Truman. Many of the famous generals were present.

When he was demobilized in 1945 he returned to the concert platform and resumed his musical adventures, which culminated in 1947 with an extensive tour of Australia and New Zealand, with Grinke acting as both leader of the Boyd Neel Orchestra and soloist. His experiences on this tour would fill a book, and he has vivid memories of sight-seeing, excited audiences and seemingly endless travel. He was delighted to find a great deal of genuine musical talent in Australia and New Zealand: some of the younger players were exceptionally gifted. All the arts seemed to be flourishing, especially painting, for which there was apparently almost more enthusiasm than for music. He could not help observing that there was the keenest interest in the works of Australasian artists.

On his return journey Grinke visited the Fiji Islands, and as soon as his identity became known to the principal medical officer he found himself being persuaded to play for the edification of native musicians. He was taken to some of their villages and fêted in a truly remarkable fashion. He was given the honour of drinking some curious concoction that tasted exactly like a solution of stomach powder but had an effect rather less salutary, and he was presented with what appeared to be rather crude tapestries. He now has them displayed in his London flat: curious cloth-like affairs of a texture resembling an inexperienced cook's attempt to do something with dried egg, and stencilled with what looks suspiciously like native versions of certain rude words.

Grinke is well known not only as a broadcaster—his playing has been transmitted from several countries, including Australia whence he broadcast the Bax concerto—but also for his many recordings for Decca. His piano trio, for instance, who enjoyed many successes in this country and abroad, have recorded the *Phantasie Trio* and the Trio No. 3 in E by John

Ireland, the *Fantasy Trio* of Frank Bridge and the Beethoven Trio in E-flat.

His solo recordings for the same company include the Vaughan Williams *Lark Ascending* and the *Concerto Accademico* (accompanied by the Boyd Neel Orchestra), a number of minor but delightful works by Dvořák for that composer's centenary, Purcell sonatas with Jean Pougnet and Dr. Boris Ord, the Mozart duos with Watson Forbes (viola), and a variety of solos accompanied by Ivor Newton, including works by Ivor Gurney, Alan Richardson, Lilli Boulanger, Smetana, Rachmaninoff, B. J. Dale and Nováček. His most recent recordings have been of the Mozart Concerto in A, the Sonata in D minor of John Ireland (with the composer at the piano), the Purcell G minor Sonata (with Arnold Goldsbrough), and the Bach Brandenburg Concertos made by the Boyd Neel Orchestra, in which he has played all the solo parts.

Grinke's repertoire is considerable, and is being extended very rapidly. It includes the works of many modern composers—chiefly British—with whom it has been his privilege to associate, frequently in the performance of their music: Benjamin Britten, Frank Bridge, John McEwen, Edmund Rubbra, Lennox Berkeley, Arthur Bliss, Alan Rawsthorne, Alan Bush, B. J. Dale, York Bowen, Theodore Holland, Arnold Fulton, Howard Ferguson, and Arnold van Wyck. It is one of his ambitions to record the Bax concerto, by the way, and it is quite likely that it will be fulfilled before this book appears in print.

In passing, it might be added that Grinke has already made an entry into the film world: he played the solo violin part in the British film *The Shop at Sly Corner*, which used extracts from the Mendelssohn Concerto.

Considering his age, Grinke's interpretative powers are quite remarkable: he can always be relied upon to play with the understanding of a scholar yet with the

W. Schimdt

HENRY HOLST

Howard Co.

FREDERICK GRINKE

verve of youth. His sound musicianship has given him an assurance that many an artist would not gain until he had passed the age of forty-five, and it is unfortunately just at that age that so many of them start to decline, generally through physical weariness. Grinke has all the attributes of a true artist, and we have every reason for anticipating great things from him now that he has taken the risk—and it *is* a risk in these days of calamitous economics—of devoting himself exclusively to solo work.

He possesses a J. B. Rogerius dated 1686, from which he draws a warm, substantial tone, employing aluminium-covered D and A, and the usual silver-covered G and steel E strings, but he frequently uses a Strad dated 1718 which has been lent to him by The Royal Academy of Music.

A stimulating personality, Grinke is broad-minded and has no fads in music. He enjoys almost every type of music, even jazz when he is in the mood for it. He considers Duke Ellington's band to be one of the best, and has always an inclination to listen to negro bands, which he finds very fascinating.

He was married in 1942 to Dorothy Sirr Sheldon, and has one son, Paul, who shares his father's enthusiasm for a ciné-camera. Grinke has made many little films on his travels, and is very proud of his "shots" of fine scenes in distant parts of the globe. He is also quite a theatre addict, by the way, and reads chiefly biography. Outdoors, he is very fond of swimming.

E

IDA HAENDEL

DURING the past ten years or so we have had the pleasure of watching Ida Haendel develop in musical virtuosity from an extremely promising child prodigy to one of the most brilliant violinists of the day. Comparatively few of the child prodigies have made such steady progress: the majority have become so blighted by early success that they have never come anywhere near artistic maturity. It has therefore been all the more gratifying to be able to witness this continual growth of artistry as Miss Haendel has come before us season after season.

She was born at Gholm, Poland, on 15 January, 1923, and took to the violin before she was four years old. Her father, an artist, was (and still is) a keen amateur musician and had no difficulty in perceiving that his daughter possessed an unusually good ear for music. So at the age of six, Ida was sent to a competent musician for instruction. She had no less than four teachers during her childhood—Mihailovitsch, and, in turn, three pupils of Carl Flesch: Frankel, Goldberg and Totenberg, all of whom spoke of Flesch in such glowing terms that she resolved to become a pupil of this master if he would accept her. Fortunately, her father had also come to the conclusion that she needed the very best teacher that Europe could provide, so shortly after her tenth birthday, he approached Carl Flesch and that eminent violinist consented to hear her.

Flesch agreed that Ida showed remarkable promise, and offered to give her lessons when, later in 1935, he went to Baden-Baden. It was he who urged her to compete in the Warsaw violin contest, which she did successfully. Then he came to London, and, in order to continue her studies, Ida came to this country. At this juncture it should be stated that lessons were also taken from two other distinguished violinists during those impressionable years: Georges Enesco and Joseph Szigeti.

After intensive training for a year or so it was arranged that Ida should play at a concert under the direction of Sir Thomas Beecham, but at the last minute it was discovered that the regulations of the London County Council did not permit a child of less than fourteen years to play at a public concert, and the engagement had to be cancelled. As soon as she reached the approved age, however, she made her début at a London concert in the Brahms concerto conducted by the late Sir Henry Wood. This, as many people will remember, was a tremendous success, and offers of further engagements began to come in almost immediately.

Her father, who had been handling her affairs with the utmost consideration for her welfare, felt strongly that she should accept only a very limited number of engagements, so that there would be ample time, not only for musical study, but for her general education, so her appearances in the concert hall were less frequent than many music-lovers would have wished.

Miss Haendel then returned to Poland for a while to give a series of concerts at a number of the larger centres in her native land, and then embarked upon a further period of study with Carl Flesch in order to perfect her technique. These lessons, with those given by Enesco and Szigeti, and the experience of concert-giving over the past five or six years, have brought her to the very high standard of musicianship that is so evident in her performances at the present time.

What is so unusual about Miss Haendel is that at the age of twenty-four she possesses a musical understanding such as few acquire before middle-age. She seems to be able to interpret each composer as if she had spent the best part of a lifetime in studying his particular works to the exclusion of everything else. She will play her Bach, Brahms and Beethoven with the insight of a scholar and then turn to something of Tchaikovsky's and give a rendering of it that will delight the most ardent devotees of Russian music. Her style generally is more robust than one would expect from a young lady, and in the more lively passages she can be as stimulating as any of those who make a speciality of musical gymnastics. Her tone is most agreeable, and seems to be acquiring quite a quality of its own.

To mention all her successes in the concert hall would, of course, be quite impossible in the short amount of space available here, but mention might be made of her splendid performance of the Dvořák and Brahms concertos in August 1946, and of the memorable farewell concert before her American tour which was given at the Albert Hall on 24 November in the same year. At this she played both the Beethoven and the new Khachaturian concertos. Her American début was made at Carnegie Hall on 29 December 1946, and her success there was repeated in all the many cities she visited during that exacting tour of the United States.

The best recording she has made up to the time of writing is that of the Tchaikovsky Concerto with the National Symphony Orchestra conducted by Basil Cameron (Decca). This was done under the new FFRR system (full frequency range recording) which gives a really faithful reproduction of the soloist's very high notes.

Miss Haendel does not follow the style of any one of the great violinists, but it is perhaps worth recording that of the living masters she admires Heifetz for sheer executive ability, Szigeti for musicianship as well as technique, and Enesco for artistry generally. She uses all four fingers on the bow, and believes that it is very bad not to do so. Her favourite concertos are those of Beethoven and Brahms, and of the contemporary composers she is drawn especially to Sibelius, William Walton, Vaughan Williams and Cyril Scott. She thinks, as do several other discriminating musicians, that Cyril Scott has been unwarrantably neglected in recent years.

She generally uses a 1726 Strad but has, on occasions, played in public upon a Guarnerius, and always uses aluminium-covered D and A strings. To keep in concert form she believes in practising twice a day—usually morning and evening—and considers that every violinist should take part regularly in chamber music: it is absolutely essential to one's musical education. There is always plenty of music-making in her home, as her father plays the 'cello, and her sister Alice is a pianist of considerable accomplishment.

In private life, Miss Haendel's interests are as varied as those of any ordinary English girl. She is very fond of outdoor life and delights in riding and swimming. The theatre is always an attraction to her, and she sees quite a number of films—Robert Donat is her favourite star. Indoors, she is always trying to beat her father at table tennis, but has, one gathers, given up trying to do so at billiards! Her literary taste is chiefly for biographies: the lives of the great are a source of unfailing fascination to her. The trouble is that it always depresses her to read of the decline and death of great composers, artists, writers, and so forth, and after finishing a biography she often feels miserable for days! One last word that will surprise many readers: Miss Haendel has a soft spot for those much-abused "outcasts" of the musical world—crooners! She thinks that some of them are quite entertaining and can provide a welcome diversion when you are in the mood for that sort of thing. A great many people pretend to despise them merely because it is considered correct to do so. Two singers of the lighter variety she specially enjoys are Anne Shelton and Bing Crosby. Whether her father, who gives the impression of being rather a strict parent, entirely approves of this is another matter!

JASCHA HEIFETZ

IT seems to be generally agreed among all who wield the bow that Jascha Heifetz is the world's greatest living violinist. There was a time when he was overshadowed by Kreisler, but now that the latter has passed his seventieth birthday there can be no doubt about the younger man's supremacy, and his veteran friend would probably be the first to admit it. Heifetz is a paragon: his interpretations are as impeccable as his phenomenal technique, in fact on one occasion Bernard Shaw felt obliged to warn him that there was a danger in being perfect. "Nothing may be perfect in this world," he told the great violinist, "or else the gods become jealous and destroy it. So you should make a habit of playing one wrong note every night before you go to bed."

Heifetz was born on 2 February 1901, in the city of Vilna, the Lithuanian capital. It is said that while he was still in his cradle his features would assume an ecstatic expression whenever he heard the sound of the fiddle played by his father, who was a member of the orchestra at the Vilna Theatre. The proud parent—Ravin Heifetz was his name—was most fascinated by his tiny son's interest in music, and would frequently play the child to sleep. We are told that the slightest discord would invariably bring an expression of disapproval on the baby's face. One or two psychologists have maintained that if a great deal of music is played to a child in its infancy it will grow up with an acute consciousness of sound, and one presumes that it will develop either a deep love of music or a determination to knife every musician it meets. (One begins to wonder what will happen in those urban areas where it is impossible to escape from the sound of neighbours' wireless sets.) However, in the case of the infant Heifetz there was little doubt that he had music in his soul, and we need not attach too much importance to these stories of his infancy.

When he was three years old his father gave him a quarter-sized fiddle for a birthday present and taught him to play a few simple tunes upon it. To the amazement of the family the boy mastered the little violin in about a week and played all manner of tunes with such taste that neighbours and friends could scarcely believe their ears. The scrapings of the average "talented child" upon a toy violin are generally a perfect misery to all who have the misfortune to come within earshot, but little Jascha rarely produced a note that was not in tune and of pleasant quality.

His father then started him upon an elementary course of study, and he made really astonishing progress, with the result that at the age of five he was allowed to enter the Imperial School of Music at Vilna. He studied with Elias Malkin, and in less than two years was able to give his first public recital. This was at Kovno, where he played the Mendelssohn concerto before an audience of over 1,000, who were quite bewitched by the smooth round tone he produced and the masterly way in which his little fingers overcame the difficulties of the last movement. His future as a child prodigy was assured.

In 1907 Vilna was visited by Leopold Auer, the famous violin professor of the St. Petersburg Conservatoire, who found his friend Malkin rhapsodizing over his phenomenal pupil. Auer had heard so many extravagant stories about child prodigies that he was heartily weary of them and did little to hide his impatience. "But you *must* hear my little Heifetz!"

Malkin insisted. Auer flatly refused: wherever he went people were thrusting little prodigies under his nose, and he had heard enough of them to last him a lifetime. Malkin then declared that he could never have heard anything like Heifetz's playing: he was really phenomenal. Auer was quite accustomed to such claims, and again refused. But Malkin persisted, and eventually Auer gave in. Heifetz and his father were called, and the lad played the Mendelssohn Concerto as coolly as if it were the first exercise in a child's instruction book. To finish his demonstration he played Paganini's Caprice No. 24, and at its conclusion Auer could restrain himself no longer: he embraced the lad, predicted a brilliant future for him, and insisted that he should come to the St. Petersburg Conservatoire without delay so that he could study under his personal guidance.

The move to St. Petersburg could not be made immediately, for it entailed a great deal of self-sacrifice on the part of Ravin Heifetz: it meant giving up his very comfortable job at the Vilna Theatre, for instance, selling up his home and going to St. Petersburg as a complete stranger. Nevertheless, arrangements were made in due course, the furniture was disposed of, and the little family set out for what was then the Russian capital.

They arrived feeling very strange, and not a little homesick. To their horror, when they called upon Auer the eminent violinist failed to remember Jascha—who was now ten years old—and regarded him as yet another child prodigy seeking "influence". He kept both father and son on the doorstep and after a few moments' demonstration of his impatience, sent them both away. Ravin was utterly dejected, but shortly afterwards approached Auer for the second time and eventually succeeded in convincing him that his son was the astonishingly brilliant child he had heard at Vilna.

Then it was discovered that no vacancies existed in Auer's class, which was already overflowing, and as the term had already started the authorities insisted that they could make no further admissions for the present. Hope was just about at its lowest ebb when Auer managed to get Jascha squeezed into the class of his assistant, Nalbandjan. Even then the boy was admitted for but a single term.

Another difficulty then arose: Jewish students of the Conservatoire were allowed to reside in St. Petersburg, but their parents were not, and it looked as if after all his sacrifices, Ravin would have to return to Vilna and leave his son alone. Fortunately, the sympathy of the Director of the Conservatoire had by this time been won, and to get over the difficulty it was arranged that Ravin should himself become a student at the Conservatoire!

Auer watched Jascha during his first six months of class work and decided that he had never known such a student in all his years as a professor. He therefore made him one of his personal pupils. It seems that the boy was put through a most comprehensive course in music, for he had to learn the piano and viola as well as his chosen instrument, and also had to become acquainted with all the other instruments of the orchestra. He was obliged to play regularly in the Conservatoire orchestra, sometimes among the first fiddles, sometimes among the seconds, and quite often with the violas. In addition, he was required to take part in many quartets, trios and other chamber ensembles. All the students were expected to make a diligent study of languages: although only Italian and Russian were supposed to be compulsory, they were also required to study French and either German or English. Heifetz was with Auer for about six years, and his master's confidence in him was such that frequently when he asked how to play a certain passage, Auer would merely wave his hand and reply with a smile: "Play it with your nose if you like: you're bound to make it sound right!"

Heifetz gave public recitals all the time he was at the Conservatoire. Soon after his admission, for instance, he played at a great open-air concert held in Odessa and drove his enormous audience of over 25,000 into a frenzy of delight. After his concluding item the crowd surged forward and both he and his parents were almost crushed to death. So one or two of the other musicians present called the police, and a stalwart officer took the little soloist to safety by concealing him under his cloak. Meanwhile, his parents had been assisted to a different exit and their anxiety was renewed when they were unable to find their son. Fortunately, with the assistance of friends and the police, the family were reunited shortly afterwards, and they went home rejoicing at what had been their son's greatest triumph to date.

While he was still a student, the fame of Jascha Heifetz spread all over Europe. He was only thirteen when he had the honour of appearing as a soloist at the Berlin Philharmonic concerts. Nikisch, the conductor, declared that never in his life had he heard such superb playing of the violin.

Offers of important engagements and nation-wide tours were now coming in so frequently that Ravin Heifetz scarcely knew how to deal with them: he was most anxious that his son's health should not be impaired by too much "concertizing". It must be said, though, that the lad stood up to the strain with remarkable fortitude.

During the early years of the Great War, Jascha's fame had aroused such interest in the United States that the most insistent demands were coming from across the Atlantic. Consequently, in the late summer of 1917, Heifetz made his first visit to America, despite the danger of a wartime crossing. He made his début at Carnegie Hall, New York, on 27 October and astounded the critics by his precocity and the purity of his tone. Journalists indulged in an orgy of purple patch writing that told the world how this sixteen-year-old boy had wrung tears from the eyes of all present, and so forth. It is true that he had been given an ovation, but the more shrewd critics saw that as he was growing out of the child prodigy class he would be required to show something more than phenomenal technique. His dazzling execution of the most preposterously difficult music was all very well, but his interpretations were quite cold compared with the more emotional playing of mature players. There was no "soul" in his Brahms and Beethoven, and one critic likened his playing of these concertos to carved marble: beautiful, but devoid of the warmth of life.

This coldness was not due entirely to Heifetz's youth. To some extent it was deliberate, because at that time he was passing through a period of strong reaction to the over-emotional playing that was characteristic of the Russian school of artists. But one may safely presume that he did not realize just how far his art had swung in the opposite direction. He was of course still very young, and one could scarcely have expected the mature conception of the artist of riper years.

This phase soon passed, for he was quite aware of his shortcomings, and his studies were from that time intensified by a sincere desire to get beneath the superficialities of technical prowess and display. During the next couple of years he acquired a new understanding of what the composer was trying to say, and his playing took on a more emotional tinge without losing any of its brilliance.

His first visit to England was made in the summer of 1920. He had by then made a number of excellent gramophone records, some 70,000 of which had already been sold in this country alone. His fame had therefore preceded him, not only by verbal and written reports of his prowess. A huge crowd of his admirers assembled to hear his first London concert, and were not disappointed, for he was careful to play only works that he knew were especially suited to his style. The better critics all spoke well of his performance, though with some reserve. The *Musical Times* of June 1920, reported:

". . . it is only possible to say, negatively, that he did nothing meretricious or that could offend fastidious taste. . . . His ease is astonishing, and the way in which even in most difficult passages he never scrapes nor scratches is all but unparalleled. His tone is strong and pure, like that of a high soprano rather than of a mezzo-soprano."

At his second London concert Heifetz played the Mendelssohn Concerto and Bach's Chaconne with less of the restraint shown on the former occasion, and made a very favourable impression. Later in the same year he returned to London again and scored another triumph with concertos by Paganini and Ernst. The critic of the *Musical Times* said the performance could rarely have been equalled for brilliancy and sheer beauty of tone in even the most difficult passages. "He plays this sort of music with a force of conviction that makes one forget that its intrinsic value is not of the highest." His playing of the César Franck Sonata in A—the sonata that Ysaÿe made famous, by the way—was less successful as he seemed somewhat out of sympathy with the mood of the work.

Then followed tours all over the world: China, Japan, Australia, India—music-lovers of all nations, near and far, clamoured to hear him, and it is said that even at this relatively early age his earnings were comparable with those of Kreisler. He had now changed from the bushy-haired youth into the reserved, sleek and fastidious artist we know to-day. Appearances are apt to be deceptive, of course, and many people do not realize that Heifetz has always been quite an athlete: he is very fond of rowing and swimming, and can play an excellent game of tennis.

Heifetz is deeply interested in the Jewish problem, and has the welfare of his race always at heart. It will be recalled that in 1925 he built an imposing concert hall at Tel-Aviv as a gift to the people of Palestine. In the same year he became a citizen of the United States, where he has lived for over a quarter of a century.

Musical education is also a subject about which he feels strongly, and he has done much to get music taught in schools as part of the general curriculum instead of being regarded as a mere "extra" subject to be taken chiefly by the more delicate children in lieu of something more strenuous. He believes that all children should be given the opportunity of learning to understand good music, for its influence upon their later lives and happiness makes it an art of great social value.

On his tours he takes his two most precious fiddles: the 1731 Strad and the 1742 Guarnerius used by Ferdinand David, but, unlike many of the other great violinists, he is keenly interested in the making of modern instruments. He advocates the utmost encouragement to makers of the present day, for they have great possibilities, and it is quite likely that some of the finest instruments of the future will have been made during the twentieth century. These makers will be less inclined to concentrate upon the construction of really first-class instruments if violinists persist in their prejudice against modern fiddles. No man is likely to make a masterpiece if he knows in advance that his work will be scorned by the better type of artist.

During the Second World War Heifetz gave dozens of concerts for the troops, in Italy and North Africa as well as in the United States. When he played in an army camp for the first time he felt more nervous than he had ever been in a concert hall, for he was afraid that the men would not be interested in his playing. So many artists had "played down" to what they imagined to be the men's level that he felt he ought to take the risk of giving them a sound classical programme. At the outset he said that whether they liked it or not he was going to start off with some Bach "because Bach is good for you!" He was well rewarded, for the men listened intently and in their applause left him in no doubt about their appreciation. At the end of the concert he asked them if they would care to make a few requests, and to his delight there were calls for "more Bach!"

Details of all his concerts for the troops cannot be given here, but a fact of some interest is that in the Middle East he gave nearly fifty recitals in two months. He played anything up to ten encores at most of them.

His magnificent recital at the Albert Hall in the autumn of 1947, when he played before the Queen and Princess Margaret and an audience of over six thousand will long be remembered. With the Royal Philharmonic Orchestra under Sir Malcolm Sargent he gave masterly performances of the Beethoven and Tchaikovsky Concertos; a deeply spiritual interpretation of the former, and a vivid, dramatic rendering of the latter.

His repertoire is vast. The concertos of Bach, Brahms, Beethoven, Mozart, Tchaikovsky, Glazounov, Sibelius, Vieuxtemps and Prokofiev are always being demanded of him, but he also gives masterly renderings of many of the less popular works, such as the Walton, which he recorded some time ago for H.M.V., the Gruenberg,[1] of which he gave the *première* in the spring of 1945 with the Philadelphia Orchestra under Eugene

[1]Louis Gruenberg (b. Russia 1884, now an American citizen) dedicated this concerto to Heifetz. It is a fascinating work employing negro spirituals.

Ormandy, and the second violin concerto of Castelnuovo Tedesco,[1] of which he gave the first performance in the spring of 1933 with the New York Philharmonic Symphony Orchestra under Toscanini.

Of his concerto recordings, the following are the better-known in this country: Beethoven's Concerto with Toscanini and the NBC Symphony Orchestra[2]: Concerto in A by Mozart (K.219) with the London Philharmonic Orchestra under John Barbirolli; the Prokofiev Concerto No. 2 in G minor with the Boston Symphony Orchestra under Kousseviztky; the Brahms Double Concerto in A minor with Emanuel Feuermann and the Philadelphia Orchestra conducted by Ormandy; the Tchaikovsky Concerto with the London Philharmonic Orchestra conducted by Barbirolli; the Walton Concerto with the Cincinnati Symphony Orchestra under Eugene Goossens; and the Brahms Concerto with the Boston Symphony Orchestra conducted by Koussevitzky.

His minor recordings are too numerous to be listed here, but mention should be made of the Saint-Saëns Introduction and Rondo Capriccioso made with John Barbirolli and the London Philharmonic Orchestra, and the César Franck Sonata in A recorded with Arthur Rubinstein at the piano. All these are H.M.V. productions.

As most violinists are aware, Heifetz has made many fine transcriptions which reveal his great ability as an editor. Some of the best of these are arrangements of the works of Debussy, Godowsky (who was also born

[1]Mario Castelnuovo-Tedesco was born in Florence in 1895 and made a considerable impression as a composer in Italy before he settled in America just before the Second World War. This second concerto is called *The Prophets* because its three movements are supposed to depict Isaiah, Jeremiah and Elijah respectively.

[2]The cadenzas Heifetz uses in the Beethoven concerto are generally supposed to be his own. This is not correct: they are by Auer and Joachim modified by Heifetz.

IDA HAENDEL

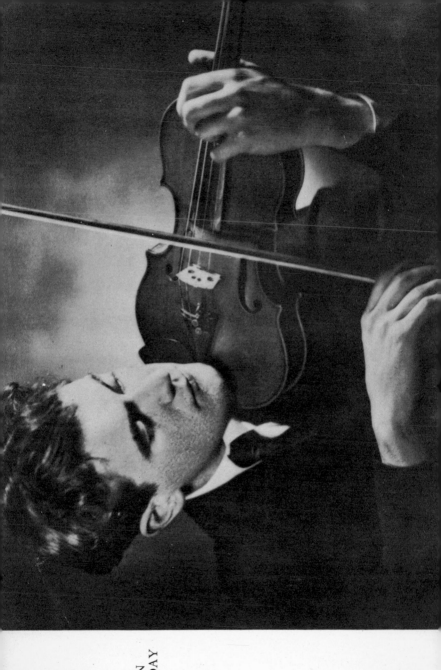

ALAN
LOVEDAY

in Vilna and later became an American citizen) and Albeniz. He has also composed a few works of some merit, and has published some popular tunes under the *nom de plume* "Jim Hoyl".

Heifetz was honoured by the French Government in 1926 when he was made a Chevalier of the Legion of Honour. Thirteen years later he was raised to the rank of Officier.

His immaculate style, which most musicians regard as the acme of perfection, has won him the allegiance of more millions than he would care to count, but it should be said that in the opinion of some critics there are certain types of music in which at least two or three other distinguished violinists can challenge his supremacy. It is perhaps significant that Nicholas Slonimsky, the eminent American musicologist (of Russian origin) still refers to him as "the virtuoso of the new school of cold tonal beauty" in his survey *Music Since 1900*. In passing, it should be noted that Heifetz does not regard himself as a paragon and is apt to take it as a doubtful compliment when people assure him that he was "born a great musician". He often points out that the greater part of his success is due to nothing more than sheer hard work.

Stories about him have been circulating in musical circles for years. One of the best concerns a certain other famous violinist who went with a pianist friend to hear Heifetz. As usual, Heifetz won a great ovation, and when at length the applause died down the other eminent violinist mopped his brow and, turning to his friend, remarked casually: "Phew! Very hot in here, isn't it?" His companion turned to him with a twinkle in his eyes and said: "Not for a pianist!"

A little anecdote that Heifetz tells against himself relates of an incident that occurred during one of his transatlantic crossings. A concert had been held on board, at which he had obliged by playing a few items, and afterwards he had played two or three

F

games of table-tennis, at which he happens to be rather good. Shortly before retiring for the night he went into the bar for a drink when a stranger approached and began rhapsodizing about his playing. "I was simply spellbound . . ." he raved, "it was one of the greatest thrills I have ever experienced . . . why, man, your back-hand return is marvellous!"

Heifetz was married[1] in 1928 to Florence Vidor of Hollywood, the film actress. There are two children, Josepha and Robert.

At home, he is a man of fairly simple tastes, though his love of art and literature as well as music is revealed in his fine collection of paintings and books. He loves to give a party, but not of the reckless cocktail type: his friends are generally expected to come prepared to share his cultural or athletic interests, and when drinks are brought round they come usually as a refreshment after an hour of chamber music or fervent discussion. The evening will quite likely end with dancing, of which the great violinist is very fond.

At his chamber music parties one is likely to meet two or three other musicians of the front rank, and they will take a delight in proving to any listeners who happen to be present that, contrary to the popular notion, eminent solo artists *can* play together in an ensemble and blend perfectly. For quartets, if they are held in Heifetz's New York flat, he will produce a table made to his own design which has music-rests illuminated so that the players can see their music while the remainder of the room is in complete darkness. This, Heifetz declares, is the ideal arrangement for chamber music, because he believes that, if possible, all music should be heard in darkness. He always likes to switch out the lights when listening to the gramophone

[1]An announcement concerning the forthcoming second marriage of Heifetz to Mrs. Francis Speilberg was made while this book was in preparation.

or a radio concert, for he maintains that the emotions aroused by music are personal, and should be kept private.

He knows that people regard him as "reserved", but that is part of his mental make-up, and he dislikes any great show of the emotions, just as he abhors the expression of "temperament" by mannerisms and eccentricities. He never goes out of his way to "make an impression" upon an audience, and that is perhaps why some people imagine that he is indifferent towards the general public. This is quite incorrect: he readily acknowledges that he is a public servant and endeavours to play the sort of music that will please the people. But that does not mean that he is under no obligation to teach them to love the best in music, and as an artist he feels compelled to improve his programmes all the time. He tries to understand his audiences, and as fast as their taste improves he gives them better and better music.

The garden of his country house is always a great joy to him and he spends many hours working in it. Unlike some of the other great musicians, he does not worry unduly about his hands: you will find him digging and weeding as unconcernedly as any country-man. And he can always find pleasure in a long country walk, especially if accompanied by his son and daughter. Heifetz also takes an interest in photography, and is not ashamed of his boyish love of a powerful car. His friends agree that he is a model of good road manners.

For many years he has been an enthusiastic patron of the cinema, but has protested over and over again at the appalling reproduction of music that comes from the talkie apparatus. For that reason he refused many very enticing offers of film contracts, and did not relent until 1939, when Samuel Goldwyn promised him personally that whatever the cost he would be recorded and reproduced in a manner acceptable to him. Heifetz then stipulated that he would appear only in the rôle of a concert violinist and under his own name, and that he would play only music that was worthy of his calling. All this was agreed, and *They Shall Have Music* was the result. Curiously enough, when this film was shown in England the reproduction of the music was far from satisfactory.

A somewhat better film from the musical point of view was *Melody of Youth*, in which Heifetz appeared and played the Saint-Saëns Introduction and Rondo Capriccioso, and the last movement of the Mendelssohn Concerto. This film was of more interest to violin students since it gave many "close-ups" of the violinist that showed his fingering and graceful bowing.

Yet another film featuring this great artist was *Carnegie Hall*, but one cannot help wondering if Heifetz is really convinced that the cinema can give even a tolerable reproduction of his art. Surely he realizes that however much trouble is taken with the recording, the music can be made a mockery by a mere mechanic when the film is being shown?

HENRY HOLST

ALTHOUGH many of us now regard him as an Englishman, Henry Holst is really of Danish origin, and it is perhaps worth recording that in Jutland he has been able to trace his ancestry back to the early part of the seventeenth century. His forbears were men of quite humble stock: fishermen, farmers, tradesmen and schoolteachers, but they all seemed to possess those qualities that produce a profound respect for arts and honest crafts. There is evidence that music played an important part in their lives, though it is true that none of them practised the art professionally.

Holst's father, for instance, was a schoolmaster, accomplished and well read, who took a keen interest in the cultural life of his village: he was the church organist, he ran a string quartet, delighted in painting and sculpture, and was an ardent booklover. He collected a library of unusual interest and size, clothing most of his treasured volumes with elegant leather bindings in his spare time. Some idea of the infinite patience with which he tooled these handsome bindings may be gained from the volumes in his son's possession to-day.

Such was the environment into which Henry Holst was born on 25 July 1899. He has many happy memories of his home in that little village of Sæby, the most vivid, perhaps, being of his father's string quartet which used the services of a fisherman as a violist and of the local chemist as a 'cellist. Music-making began as soon as the day's work was done, and Holst can distinctly remember how the violist would come straight from his boat and play, with the fish-scales still adhering to his fingers. Many a time was young Henry allowed to stay up late, or even to come down from bed, to hear them play something that he particularly liked.

He was therefore given every encouragement in his interest in music, and as soon as he was old enough, his father gave him a good grounding in the art of playing the fiddle. Unfortunately, this able parent died in 1907 so he knew nothing of the success that his son was to enjoy in the musical profession.

In 1913 Henry Holst was sent to the Royal Conservatoire at Copenhagen, where for four years he was privileged to study the violin under Axel Gade, son of Niels Gade (1817-1890) the Danish composer, and the piano and harmony under Carl Nielsen (1865-1931). He made his début at the age of eighteen in the same city, playing—among other things—the first concerto of Vieuxtemps and the Brahms Sonata in G. This concert aroused considerable enthusiasm, and several of the critics predicted a brilliant future for him.

Shortly afterwards, that famous Hungarian violinist, Telmanyi, visited Copenhagen and was approached on Holst's behalf by Gade, who felt that the young artist could benefit substantially by a period of instruction from the distinguished visitor. (The willingness with which the Danish teacher was prepared to hand over his most promising pupil was typical of the way in which he invariably put his pupils' interests before his own.) Telmanyi gave Holst an audition, agreed that he was indeed a gifted young man, and accepted him for a year's training. This was followed by a visit to Germany, where Holst studied with Willy Hess (1859-1939) for a while. This further period of instruction with one of Germany's finest violinists (a pupil of Joachim) encouraged Holst to compete for the leadership of the Berlin Philharmonic Orchestra, which became vacant at about that time and was to be filled by open competition. He was one of the fifteen competent young violinists chosen for the final contest, and was extremely gratified when the decision was announced in his favour. One of the test pieces, he recalls, was the Ernst Concerto in F-sharp minor: a work rarely, if ever, heard nowadays.

So in 1923 Henry Holst became the leader of one of the finest orchestras in the world, and for the next eight years enjoyed the wonderful experience of playing an exceptionally large repertoire under almost every conductor of fame. For a naturally gifted musician such experience during the impressionable "twenties" was bound to cause an unusually rapid development of his artistic nature, and as soon as he began to appear as a soloist many people remarked upon the depth of his understanding of not only the classics but a vast amount of modern music as well. It was a very strenuous life, of course, but one full of interest and excitement.

It was perhaps inevitable that sooner or later Holst should have longed for artistic independence. However delightful it may be to play under such dominant individuals as Bruno Walter, Furtwängler, Mengelberg and so forth, there comes a time when the artist within any strong personality desires self-expression beyond the very limited scope afforded by orchestral playing. In 1931, therefore, Holst decided to follow a more independent path, and with some reluctance no doubt, resigned his appointment.

Arthur Catterall had recently relinquished his professorship at the Royal Manchester College of Music, and when this position was offered to Holst, the young Danish violinist decided to accept it, discounting, as Charles Hallé had done some eighty years previously, the popular notion about the average Englishman's philistine attitude towards music.

Over fourteen years were to be spent in that dampish city that has contributed so much to British music, and during that period Holst travelled extensively in the northern counties as a soloist, very often with the Hallé Orchestra. Much could be written about his experiences in that enthusiastic part of England, but it must suffice to say that the one quality he admired above all others in the northern music-lovers was their great loyalty and kindness to any really competent artist who was prepared to spend the greater part of his life in serving the musical interests of the North.

Looking back over those years, Holst can recall some exceedingly gratifying experiences, as, for instance, that memorable occasion in 1933 when with the Hallé Orchestra under Sir Thomas Beecham, he gave one of the finest performances of the Sibelius Concerto we have ever been privileged to hear. Then there was the first European performance of the Walton Concerto in 1941, which he gave with the Royal Philharmonic Society. This concerto, by the way, he has now played over twenty-five times.

In 1945 Henry Holst left Manchester to take up a professorship at the Royal College of Music, London, and in the past year or two has figured prominently in the musical life of the capital, not only as a soloist and teacher but as leader of that accomplished ensemble known as the Philharmonia Quartet, which was formed in 1941 to make recordings for Columbia. In this he is associated with Ernest Element (second violin), Herbert Downes (viola) and Anthony Pini ('cello).

The Philharmonia Quartet's recordings include the Mozart Quartet No. 17 in B-flat major (*The Hunt*)[1]; the Beethoven in F major, Opus 59, No. 1 (*Rasoumof-fsky*)[2]; the Schubert No. 14 in D minor (*Death and the Maiden*)[2]; and the Mozart Quintet for Clarinet and

[1] In this recording the second violin part is played by Jean Pougnet and the viola by Frederick Riddle.

[2] In this recording the second violin part is played by D. Wise and the viola by Frederick Riddle.

Strings in A major (K.581) made with Reginald Kell.

Other recordings in which Henry Holst has taken part are of the Haydn Trio No. 1 in G major (with Eileen Joyce, piano, and Anthony Pini, 'cello); the Dvořák Trio in E minor (with Louis Kentner, piano, and Anthony Pini, 'cello); and the Beethoven *Arch-Duke* Trio No. 7 in B-flat major (with Solomon, piano, and Anthony Pini, 'cello). All these are Columbia recordings, with the exception of the last, which is H.M.V.

Holst's tours abroad have taken him over the greater part of Europe, and he has made a very favourable impression in such countries as Norway, Sweden, Denmark, Holland and Hungary, with a repertoire that has included the concertos of Busoni, Elgar, Walton and Sibelius as well as the more widely-known classics. His favourite concertos, incidentally, are the Sibelius, Brahms and Elgar, and it is perhaps of interest to note that on the Third Programme recently he broadcast a concerto by his compatriot Carl Nielson.

The outstanding feature of Holst's playing is undoubtedly the fullness of tone which frequently gives one a sense of great mastery, especially in such works as the Sibelius and Elgar concertos. His unusually strong and steady bow arm enables him to execute forceful passages very impressively, and he can always be relied upon to make the most of anything vigorous. This somewhat muscular style seems in keeping with what one might call his "massive" interpretation of certain concertos. He is always stimulating—a trifle too vigorous for some people, perhaps—and frequently manages to bring out something in his tone that other players seem to miss. Technically, he appears to lack nothing.

Of his fellow artists there are three whom he admires in particular: Heifetz for his superbly immaculate and elegant playing, Szigeti for his intellect, great range and interesting choice of music, and Menuhin for sound technique and many glorious attributes in tone and interpretation.

His taste in music is comprehensive, and he enjoys everything that is good—even dance music. Just as he loves the waltzes of Strauss, for instance, he can also appreciate polkas, tangos and modern dance tunes if they serve a useful purpose. He is always reluctant to say what is good or bad in music, for he feels that this is a matter that is largely decided by one's personal taste. "If one gets pleasure out of music at a given moment," he declares, "it fulfils its purpose, and might therefore be regarded as good."

The teaching of music is a matter to be taken very seriously, he feels, and believes that because it is so essential that pupils should be able to hear their playing as others hear it, the studio of the modern teacher should be equipped with a recording apparatus so that after a pupil has played, say, a concerto (with his master playing the orchestral part upon the piano), he can listen critically to his own playing and note all the faults. It is a well-known fact that when at first they listen to their own recordings, the majority of inexperienced musicians can scarcely recognize their own playing! The pupil must know exactly how the music *should* sound before he attempts to play it, and therefore he should take every opportunity of listening to the recordings of the great violinists if he is unable to hear them in person. A pupil who can "hear mentally", as it were, a concerto he is about to perform, will play it almost subconsciously. Private recordings, or "playbacks" as they are generally called, can also be extremely useful in comparing one's own interpretation of a work with those of other artists.

Henry Holst has observed that in this country technical perfection is demanded in an artist before "soulful insight". However deeply one understands a work, a British audience will give little credit unless it is played faultlessly; in other words, they will tolerate an uninspired rendering, but not one marred by a wrong note. Therefore, he urges the young artist in England to strive first towards technical perfection and then to add something if he can. England, he feels, is a very educative country for the solo artist because of this extreme love of flawless playing. Our critics, too, are apt to be very severe.

To those who are troubled by "nerves", he would say that regular practice, systematic memory training, and, above all, an understanding of the psychological side of playing are three essentials in gaining confidence. He finds that the morning hours and late evening are the best for practising.

Like most other solo violinists, Holst uses aluminium-covered G and D strings, but until very recently always preferred a gut A. Now, however, he prefers a nylon A. (Nylon strings, being American, are extremely difficult to get, and Mr. Holst volunteers no information upon the ways and means of obtaining them in this country!) He uses a Guarnerius del Gesù dated 1742, but also possesses a fine Joseph Rocca 1825.

Henry Holst was married in 1926 to Else Werner of Copenhagen, daughter of the eminent nature photographer. They have two daughters, Ingelise aged twenty, and Helle who is twelve. Their home is in Kensington.

His recreations are tennis, cycling, sea- and sun-bathing and lounging in a comfortable armchair with a good book near at hand. He is fond of reading history —musical history for preference.

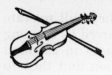

FRITZ KREISLER

THROUGHOUT the world, the name of this veteran violinist is familiar even to those who make no claim to knowledge of musical matters. His appearances nowadays are rare, but he will long be remembered as a fine artist with a delightful personality and, strangely enough, one of the smallest and most curious repertoires ever possessed by a violinist who succeeded in winning the respect of the critics. In the history of music he will also take a minor place as a composer of many pleasant little pieces for his instrument and as the perpetrator of a hoax that fooled the musical pundits for years.

Fritz Kreisler was born on 2 February 1875, in Vienna, son of an eminent physician of that city. His father, an enthusiastic amateur musician, taught him to play the fiddle when he was very young, but found in him a most reluctant pupil: the boy showed amazing aptitude, but was not at all keen to practise. He positively loathed "exercises". Nevertheless, parental encouragement was strong, and by the time he was seven he had become such an accomplished little player that he was invited to appear at a public concert with Carlotta Patti (sister of Adelina Patti). The outstanding success of this concert, at which he played a variety of little pieces with impeccable taste, made his parents decide to send him to the Vienna Conservatoire forthwith. On applying for his admission, however, they discovered that the rules of the institution precluded students under fourteen years of age, but they eventually managed to persuade the authorities that the lad's talent was such as would justify a special exception to the regulations, and he was admitted without further delay.

The young Fritz had been using one or two quite ordinary little fiddles up to this time—the first had been made out of a cigar box, we are told— but when he first went to the Conservatoire he was presented with a half-sized Thiers, which he used for several years, and to win the gold medal. To celebrate this early success he was given a three-quarter-sized Amati by a few of his friends, but it was rather a disappointment to him because he felt that he had become entitled to a full-sized instrument.

At the Vienna Conservatoire he studied for three years with Joseph Hellmesberger, and at the end of that period won the gold medal mentioned in the preceding paragraph. In those days he was rather under the spell of Joachim, whose playing he greatly admired, and he was also inspired by that brilliant and celebrated pianist Anton Rubinstein.

Then he went to the Paris Conservatoire to make a further study of the violin with Massart and to master the intricacies of theoretical subjects under Delibes. He was by that time a great deal more interested in music generally, but still found the utmost difficulty in practising patiently: many a time was he tempted to rebel against the drudgery of exercises, which, he felt, took all the pleasure out of music. He invariably devoted far less time to practice than that prescribed by his teacher, but in spite of this neglect, he won the Premier Grand Prix while he was still in his twelfth year, even though he was the youngest of forty contestants.

After about another year of study—chiefly in Rome —he met Moritz Rosenthal, the pianist, and they planned to tour together. Their decision to visit America was a bold one, for Fritz was still only thirteen and had not yet established himself in Europe, but the experience was to prove useful in later life. His début took place at the Steinway Hall, New York, on 9 November 1888, and was quite successful. One critic declared that the young violinist was a musician to his finger-tips, and predicted that hard work and a few more years' experience would put him in the vanguard of his profession, but the majority looked upon him merely as yet another child prodigy, and their remarks did little to indicate the prospects of the young artist. These moderate successes and mild notices of approval by critics who did not take him seriously were a great disappointment to both Fritz and his parents, and consequently, on their return to Europe it was decided the he would have to prepare for some other profession. This decision was supported by his rejection by the Vienna Philharmonic Orchestra when he applied for a humble post as a second violinist.

Fritz Kreisler was accordingly sent to the Vienna Gymnasium to study medicine. It is to his credit that he went willingly and applied himself with great diligence, but it soon became apparent that he was not meant to heal the sick, and his next move was to Paris —to study art. Now his interest in painting had always been competing against his music, and it was quite a good plan, in those impressionable years, to give it a chance to flower. We are told that as an art student under Julien he "shaped well", and that several other responsible artists spoke enthusiastically of his prospects. Meanwhile he retained his interest in music, but his violin ceased to attract him altogether.

We are so accustomed to regard Kreisler as a wealthy man that it is difficult to realize that in those days he was extremely poor. When he left Paris he decided to study painting for a while in Rome, and to do so had to exist chiefly on oranges and water! He loved the student life of Rome very nearly as much as the Bohemian existence he had enjoyed in Paris, but it was not long before he was entertaining doubts about a career as an artist. His period of compulsory military service was then approaching, and to the surprise of his friends he started preparing for a difficult army examination to get a commission. This he passed fairly easily, and in due course found himself in a regiment of Uhlans. During the ensuing year he left his violin severely alone and took his military duties with the utmost seriousness.

When he returned to civilian life the question of his career became one of paramount importance: he could not go on changing his mind for ever. So with some reluctance—this is his own admission, by the way —he turned once again to his violin. As one would imagine, he found that it was not at all easy to pick up the threads again: he had lost the suppleness of his fingers, and he discovered to his dismay that his technique generally had become very rusty. There was no alternative but sheer hard work. He went into the country for eight weeks and practised continually for lengthy periods every day. On his return he was overjoyed when everybody told him that he was better than ever before: his playing was quite as good as when he visited America and he seemed to have a more mature understanding of the music.

Then began the wearisome task of "getting known", of convincing the impresarios, of pleasing the more influential critics and so forth. What a struggle it was! There seemed to be so many other brilliant young artists competing for the public's favour, so many people with "big names" available for engagement, and so few who were willing to give him a reasonable hearing. The years 1895 to 1903 were one long struggle for recognition, and it is significant that in his own opinion he played quite as well then as in those later years when he was a public idol. His first important success was in 1899 when he made a brilliant début in Berlin

playing concertos by Max Bruch and Vieuxtemps and
Paganini's *Non più mesta* variations. Even then the
majority of the critics completely failed to assess his
greatness as an artist: only one or two perceived that
a new virtuoso had arrived.

Later in the same year he made another visit to
America, and this time his reception was very much
better, for his interpretations of Bach, Beethoven and
Brahms made a deep impression. This was indeed
encouraging, but more disappointments were in store
for him. His first visit to England in the spring of
1901, for instance, was utterly depressing. He spent
weeks in London trying to get a hearing, but nobody
seemed at all keen to engage him. Eventually, he made
his début here at one of Richter's concerts on 12 May,
and was scarcely noticed.

It was America that gave him the greatest encouragement, and his decision to visit that country again in
1902 changed the whole course of his life, for on his
outward journey he met a beautiful, red-headed, young
American lady named Harriet Lies. They fell in love
at first sight and the bold young musician lost no time
in asking her to marry him. Alas! her father, a wealthy
tobacco merchant, was not at all keen on his daughter
marrying "a mere fiddler", particularly one whose
prospects were still rather uncertain, but love prevailed,
and the two were married in the following November.
A more suitable wife could scarcely be imagined, and
Kreisler has never ceased to praise her remarkable
intellect and uncanny intuition, which, he says, has
helped him over all life's difficulties. She has always
been "a great inspiration" to him.

His fame was now spreading rapidly. He visited all
the countries of Europe, establishing himself as one of
the finest living violinists, and in London on 19 May
1904—only a few years after his dismal experiences
here—he was presented with the Philharmonic Society's
coveted gold medal. Success followed success, and a

NONA LIDDELL

FRITZ
KREISLER

typical example of the praise he now received may be
found in a report of one of the Queen's Hall concerts
at which he appeared under the direction of Sir (then
Mr.) Henry Wood. It is from *The Strad* of December
1905, and runs: ". . . before an enormous audience Herr
Kreisler played, as one inspired, Mozart's Concerto in
A and Viotti's in A minor, No. 22. The performances
were quite superb for the beauty alike of tone, technique and temperament, while no violinist alive or
dead has or could have had a more distinguished
style."

No useful purpose would be served by recording all
his many triumphs during the next few years, so we
may pass on to the year 1914, when the declaration of
war came as a great shock to Kreisler while he was on
holiday in Switzerland. His love of his native country,
and of Vienna in particular, would not allow him to
waver for an instant, and he proceeded at once to rejoin
his old regiment. He was stationed first in Galicia, and
was soon to find that army life in wartime was very
different from that experienced during his peacetime
training: he learned for the first time in his life what
it was like to sleep in a bed of mud. A violent contrast
to the comfortable and glamorous life of a travelling
virtuoso! These experiences made such a vivid impression upon him that he afterwards published them
in book form.[1]

On 6 September 1914 he was engaged in resisting
a Russian cavalry attack when a lance pierced his foot
and he was taken to hospital. Although the injury was
not very serious the authorities decided that his days as
a soldier were over, and he was discharged shortly
afterwards. He then began giving recitals in aid of
war charities and sold his famous Strad so that he could
give all the money to swell the proceeds of these concerts.
For the same cause he embarked upon another tour of

[1] *Four Weeks in the Trenches: the War Story of a Violinist.*

G

America, this time taking an instrument worth only 300 dollars.

It was of course inevitable that America's entry into the war should arouse violent antagonism towards him, and he was obliged to withdraw entirely from public life. He settled in Maine and spent most of his time in gardening.

Any fears he might have had about a continuation of this hostile attitude after the war were dispelled when he resumed his career with a concert at Carnegie Hall, New York, in 1919, for on this occasion he received one of the greatest ovations he had ever known. Similarly, he was given a tremendous welcome when he appeared in London again at the Queen's Hall on 4 May 1921. And, as everybody knows, his concerts during the next two decades brought joy to countless millions all over the earth. His world tours established him as the most celebrated and popular—and the most highly-paid— violinist of the century.

A point of great interest in those days was his habit of entertaining the vast audiences at his more "popular" concerts with a variety of pleasant little pieces—some of them were quite trifling—which he introduced as transcriptions from the works of such composers as Couperin, Martini, Vivaldi, Francoeur, etc. This practice went unquestioned until the eminent American critic Olin Downes tried to trace the origin of the Praeludium and Allegro that Kreisler had been playing as his own transcription of Pugnani. Finding nothing like it among the works of this composer, Downes challenged Kreisler on the subject. Previously, when asked about such works, the great violinist had said that he discovered them in various old monasteries of Europe in which he had done musical research, but on this occasion Downes was very persistent in his inquisition, and eventually, Kreisler confessed that all these works were his own composition. On 7 February

1935, he cabled from Venice the following confession to the *New York Times*: "The entire series labelled 'classical manuscripts' are my original compositions with the sole exception of the first eight bars from the Couperin *Chanson Louis XIII*, taken from a traditional melody. Necessity forced this course upon me thirty years ago when I was desirous of enlarging my programmes. I found it inexpedient and tactless to repeat my name endlessly on the programmes."

This confession caused a great sensation in the musical world, and many of the critics attacked Kreisler violently. The hoax was unparalleled in the history of music, for while some composers had adopted pseudonyms (the late Sir Henry Wood, for instance, adopted that of Paul Klenovsky for his arrangement of the Bach D minor Toccata and Fugue) none had tried to pass off his works as those of an acknowledged master. Naturally, those who most resented the hoax were the musicologists who had been fooled by the great violinist's action. Kreisler defended himself with the argument that as a young man he found that nobody would listen to his compositions, but as soon as he attached recognized names to them, they were immediately accepted as minor classics! On one occasion he played his *Liebesfreud*, *Liebesleid*, and *Schön Rosmarin* as transcriptions of pieces by Josef Lanner, together with his own *Caprice Viennois*, and was roundly abused by a well-known Austrian critic for his audacity in daring to group one of his own trifles with works of Lanner! Why should a mere label transform a trifling work into a classic?

To be quite fair, it must be said that a few critics took his hoax in good part, and even acknowledged that he had taught the musical world—or shall we say, musical snobdom—a much-needed lesson, but for several years afterwards the great violinist was regarded with undisguised hostility in certain quarters.

When Hitler annexed Austria, Kreisler applied for, and received, French nationality, but for many years he has made his home in America, and in May 1943, he accepted American citizenship.

In April 1941, he was involved in a street accident in which he sustained severe injuries to his head. He was in hospital for six weeks, during which time he received many thousands of letters and telegrams from all over the world, and well over a hundred offers of blood transfusions. When he returned to public life in November 1942 and gave a concert in New York, his huge audience rose from their seats to greet him. During the next few years much of his time was spent in giving recitals to wounded men of the American army and navy.

Throughout the greater part of his life Kreisler disliked broadcasting, and consequently was unheard by many millions who were unable to attend his concerts. Not until the summer of 1944 did he modify his views, and this was only after he had given a series of recitals and heard recordings played back to him. Then he said that he was satisfied that he had learned "microphone technique" and was prepared to make further broadcasts occasionally. According to one report, sums substantially in excess of 5,000 dollars have been offered to him for a single half-hour broadcast.

His occasional concerts nowadays are always accorded a place of honour in America's musical calendar, and they are often in support of some good cause, as, for instance, the remarkable performance he gave in New York in 1946 at a concert in memory of the late President Roosevelt. Over 100,000 dollars was raised for the fund to combat infantile paralysis. Some months later he gave a recital at Atlanta, Georgia, that drew the largest audience ever known in that city.

The first full-sized fiddle Kreisler used was the Gand-Bernadel presented to him by the Paris Conservatoire when he won the Grand Prix de Rome, but he was rather disappointed in its tone. A few years later, his father gave him a Grancino, which he used for the next seven or eight years. Then he acquired from a friend a damaged instrument that had been taken in part payment of a debt, and believing it to be a fiddle of exceptionally good tone, he had it repaired. To his great joy it proved to be a genuine Gagliano, and after only a small amount of attention it became one of the most serviceable instruments he had ever possessed. He used it continually until 1905, when he bought a superb Guarnerius which he played for a couple of years. Then he discovered another fiddle of the same make, but of superior tone, and tried to buy it. Unfortunately, it had just been sold to a collector, but, determined to acquire it, Kreisler sought out this gentleman and begged permission to play it. The collector agreed readily, and being very moved by the great artist's performance, said that anyone who could draw such lovely tone from the instrument ought to possess it: so he sold it to Kreisler for £2,000. This exquisite fiddle is dated 1737, and has the maker's initials set in diamonds on the tailpiece. The pegs and buttons are similarly decorated, and its silver case is richly overlaid. The tone is very sweet indeed, but it seems to be a somewhat temperamental instrument, and one must understand its peculiarities in order to get the best out of it. Kreisler also possesses two or three other fiddles of great value. His famous "Lord Amherst" Strad was sold recently to Jacques Gordon of the Eastman School of Music.

His style of playing is quite individual; it is full of romantic charm, full-bodied and typically Viennese, but at times one detects almost an English virility. His tone is warm and glowing, and his superb artistry becomes especially apparent in unaccompanied passages, for his intonation is perfect and he displays great feeling for the music. His profound cultural background has undoubtedly deepened his artistic perception. A musician, he believes, should possess a sound knowledge and understanding of art generally, otherwise he is bound to be at a disadvantage in trying to express his feelings in music. "Those who are interested in nothing but their own art are not great artists," he maintains.

Kreisler is most interested in chamber music, and has written a string quartet, but has never pretended to achieve anything as an ensemble player. He did appear in public once as a member of a string quartet, but the result was not very satisfactory. He is also an accomplished pianist, but again, never plays the piano in public.

Apart from his many compositions for the violin, he has written two pleasant operettas, *Apple-blossoms* (first performed in New York in 1919) and *Sissy* (a moderate success in Vienna in 1923), and the music for the film *The King Steps Out*. Many of his arrangements of classical and modern music are well known.

Several of his recordings are of his own violin pieces, such as the *Rondino on a theme of Beethoven*, *Schön Rosmarin*, *Liebesfreud*, *Liebesleid*, *Caprice viennois*, *Tambourin chinois*, etc., but he has also recorded a number of his excellent arrangements of little pieces by classical and modern composers for H.M.V., as well as the Mozart Concerto in D, the Beethoven, Brahms and Mendelssohn, with the London Philharmonic Orchestra. With Zimbalist he has also made a good recording of the Bach Concerto for two violins in D minor.

There can be no doubt that Kreisler's strong personality has contributed to his enormous popularity: his bearing on the platform and that kindly smile have done much to win the favour of his audiences. His generosity, too, will long be remembered. After the Great War, for instance, he gave the greater part of his income to the alleviation of distress in his native Austria, and his wife undertook personal responsibility for over forty war orphans. For five years he contributed handsomely towards the support of 1,500 starving artists.

Many other musicians have reason to be grateful to him for kindly acts and assistance in times of need. An example of the sort of thing he used to do will be found in an incident that took place during one of his visits to Dublin. Walking along one of the main streets in very bad weather he was vexed to hear a talented young lady playing the violin in the gutter. He stood for a few minutes listening as she played in the rain, and then told her that he would find her a job. Of course, he had no idea how to start this undertaking, but he did not rest until he had secured for her a permanent post in a theatre orchestra.

He has always been unmoved by the favours and patronage of royalty, and showed little enthusiasm for their invitations unless they happened to be genuinely interested in music. On the other hand, he has invariably been keen to meet great scientists, philosophers, painters and writers when on his travels, whether they have been interested in music or not. His interest in science, medicine and surgery is well known, but few of his admirers realize that he can speak no fewer than eight modern languages, and has also a good knowledge of Latin and Greek. Incidentally, he is a fervent collector of rare books.

His spontaneous wit makes him an ever-welcome guest at the houses of his many friends, and he delights in good company, but he loathes invitations to play at private parties held by prominent members of society. In his earlier days, particularly when he was in his prime as a virtuoso, he received dozens of such invitations and tried to discourage people from sending them by charging very high fees. On one occasion a fabulously wealthy lady demanded his services, and would not be deterred even when he quoted a fee of 3,000 dollars for playing just a few little pieces. So he accepted the engagement. The lady then told him that she did not wish him to mix with her guests, many of whom would be very prominent people, and he replied immediately: "In that case, madam, my fee will be only 2,000 dollars."

Kreisler has never overcome his dislike of practising, and even when he was giving regular concerts he never did more than three hours a day. During those years it was his wife who kept him up to concert pitch, for if he began to neglect his practising she would literally drive him to it! While on holiday he would not touch his fiddle for weeks on end.

He has always held the opinion that too much practising is apt to cramp one's style, and that many musicians worry so much about technique that they tend to lose sight of the character of the music they are trying to interpret. The hands should be regarded as of secondary importance, for after all, they are but executive organs of the mind. Kreisler has for many years maintained that the suppleness of the fingers, about which so many musicians are perpetually concerned, can be maintained as easily by three minutes' immersion in hot water as by a couple of hours of wearisome practice—provided, of course, that one is playing fairly regularly.

He has no unusual methods to which he attributes his extraordinary success, and any attempt to "draw him out" on this subject generally results in a tribute to his wife, to whom, he declares, he owes everything. " But for her," he says, " I should be but an obscure member of an orchestra."

NONA LIDDELL

ON the threshold of what promises to be quite a brilliant career as a solo violinist is Nona Liddell, whose playing has already won the commendation of several of our leading musicians. Many young players with good technique seem to be full of promise in their student days, but fail to fulfil the hopes of their friends when they get out into the world, so one hesitates to predict the future of any of these "stars of to-morrow." But the case of Nona Liddell is rather different because she seems to be more than a violinist with a fine technique: she is a young musician of intellect, and has a personality that is already showing itself behind the inevitable modesty of a young lady just out of her 'teens.

She was born in Ealing in 1927 and started playing the fiddle when she was five. Her mother had been a student at the Royal College of Music and had done quite a lot of teaching in India. For nine years Nona Liddell was a pupil of Miss Jessie Grimson, and then at the age of fourteen went for a year as a private pupil of Rowsby Woof. At sixteen she won the Ada Lewis Scholarship to the Royal Academy of Music, where she studied for two terms under Marjorie Hayward and the remainder of the time under Paul Beard.

Miss Liddell's general education was received at the Notting Hill and Ealing High School. A point of interest is that when she made her début at a Promenade concert in the summer of 1947 she appeared in the same programme as Astra Desmond, the singer, who went to the same school. Throughout her schooldays Miss

Liddell's chief interest was dramatic art, and she spent a great deal of time in organising and taking part in amateur theatricals. The only prize she ever won was, oddly enough, for sight-singing. Her best and favourite subjects at school were History, English and French.

Nona Liddell's first professional engagement of any importance was in 1943, when she was about sixteen. This was at a concert held at the Wygeston Grammar School, Leicester, in which she played, among other things, three movements of the Lalo *Symphonie Espagnole* and the Tartini G minor Sonata.

At the Academy she played an enormous amount of chamber music which, she now feels, was largely responsible for the excellent progress she made during those years. She also feels very indebted to Paul Beard for his splendid training and kindly assistance. Much of the sonata playing she did in those days was with the late Rae Leeming, a fellow student.

Her favourite concertos are the Sibelius and Brahms, both of which she played with the Academy Orchestra under Clarence Raybould before she left that establishment in 1947, but she is also a great lover of Bach, whose architectural splendour, she feels, outshines even the noble symphonies of Beethoven. Most modern music appeals strongly to her, and she is making a special study of it, particularly the works of William Walton and Benjamin Britten.

In March 1947 Miss Liddell went to Brussels with a party of Academy students as the violin soloist. At the Conservatoire they gave an interesting concert, with Miss Liddell contributing such items as the Delius Second Sonata and Ronald Smith's *Légende* for violin and piano.

It is perhaps too early to say much about Nona Liddell's style, but she has considerable technical ability and interprets with understanding. It is interesting to note that she admires Ginette Neveu for the "virility" of her playing, for her sincerity and great artistry in subordinating her phenomenal technique for the music's sake. Szigeti is admired for his superb playing of the classics, and Frederick Grinke for his sound musicianship and sensitive playing. She uses a Testore dated 1733 and prefers a gut A string to the more modern metal-covered type.

Miss Liddell is a voracious reader of fiction, history, biography and mythology—especially Finnish mythology because of her great interest in the life and works of Sibelius. Her favourite authors are Galsworthy, Somerset Maugham, Dickens, and all the Elizabethan and Jacobean playwrights. She is still a keen theatre-goer and is fond of art, but realizes that her knowledge of it is very limited. She is tolerant towards dance music, jazz and "swing"[1], but is not an *habituée* of the ballroom. Out of doors she favours swimming and sailing as recreations.

She has two sisters: Olwen, a pianist, and Hilary, an actress whose love of the stage enables her to stand the racket of working in a repertory company not far from London and travelling nearly a hundred miles a day.

[1]It seems that these three terms are not synonymous!

ALAN LOVEDAY

WE come now to the youngest of all the artists portrayed in this book: Alan Loveday, that remarkable young man from New Zealand who caused quite a sensation in the summer of 1946, when as a lad of eighteen he made his first important public appearance in this country at the People's Palace.

He was born at Palmerston North, New Zealand, on 29 February 1928 — superstitious people will no doubt be able to connect this date in some way with his "leap" to success—and started to play the fiddle at the age of three on a one-eighth size instrument made specially for him. His father was for many years a professional violinist and was therefore his teacher until he came to England, while his mother made herself responsible for his general education.

When he was about nine years of age he was heard by the Budapest String Quartet, who were making a tour of New Zealand, and they were so impressed by his unusual skill that they gave a benefit performance in his home town to start a fund for his training in England. A small committee was formed, consisting of the Mayor and other prominent local people, and by 1939 sufficient money had been raised to send Alan to London.

The year in which the Second World War broke out was not an auspicious one for the arrival of an unknown young violinist in this country, but he had the good fortune to meet Albert Sammons some time afterwards, and that eminent artist at once perceived in

him the makings of a fine violinist. He accepted him
as a private pupil, and in due course Alan Loveday was
awarded a scholarship to the Royal College of Music,
where he was able to continue studying under Sammons's
guidance.

Most people regard Loveday's appearance at the
People's Palace in 1946 as his début, but he actually
played in public on two or three occasions before this,
one of them being quite early in the war when he played
the Mendelssohn Concerto at Worthing with Albert
Sammons conducting. This, by the way, was one of
the very few concerts at which Sammons wielded a
baton instead of a bow.

An important milestone in Loveday's career was
his splendid performance of the Tchaikovsky Concerto
at a Promenade concert during the summer of 1946.
This brought him not only the acclamation of a delighted
audience but praise from some of our most distinguished
critics. One of them, writing in *The Strad*, referred to
his "beautiful velvety tone produced without apparent
effort" and the purity of his intonation. The latter is
an important point, because one of Loveday's finest
accomplishments is his ability to play a beautiful note,
absolutely in tune, even in the dizziest harmonic heights.
This is something that cannot always be said about
certain violinists of international repute.

From that time, Loveday has been favoured with
a number of important engagements, including further
Promenade concerts, about fifteen or sixteen with the
Liverpool Philharmonic Orchestra under such conductors as Sir Malcolm Sargent and Dr. Reginald Jacques,
and at least three with the Hallé Orchestra under John
Barbirolli. So far, most of his appearances have been
in the northern counties, but with broadcast recitals
and future concert performances in London he is likely
to become a favourite all over Great Britain before he
is much older. He certainly has everything in his

favour—his left hand is really quite remarkable—and he requires only that "polish" that a few more years' experience will undoubtedly bring, together with an improved *vibrato*, to establish himself in the front rank of solo violinists.

Alan Loveday attributes his early success to good training when he was very young. He uses all his fingers on the bow, and seems to have no fads or "precious" notions about violin-playing. His love of Bach is as fervent as that of a young organist raised in an English cathedral, but his favourite concerto is the Mozart Violin Concerto No. 5 in A major (K.219) which, of course, is included in his own repertoire with those of Bach, Brahms, Beethoven, Mendelssohn, Elgar, Sibelius and others.

His "ideal" violinist is Heifetz, and he never tires of listening to the records made by that master. In practising, Loveday finds that he can make better progress by doing short, irregular periods than by setting himself definite sessions of work. Lengthy practising, however doggedly it is pursued, he considers to be inadvisable.

In person he is typical of any other normal young man of his age: he would far rather cycle in the lanes of Sussex, where he lives, than spend his time in courting the favour of the musical snobs. One could scarcely find a more frank and unaffected musician. A million other youths with his ability would have acquired at least one pair of pink velvet trousers to go with it. Watch him playing cricket or tennis and you will feel glad that musicians no longer have to cultivate long hair and unhealthy complexions in order to make an "artistic" impression. Typical, too, is his candour in acknowledging that he enjoys listening to dance music. He is keen to see the world, and it is one of his ambitions that he will be able to tour his native New Zealand, Australia and America.

THOMAS MATTHEWS

A BRILLIANT English violinist of whom we hear far too little, for some mysterious reason, is Thomas Matthews: an artist of great technical skill.

He was born at Birkenhead on 9 May 1907, nephew of J. E. Matthews, an accomplished violinist who used to lead the orchestra attached to Sir Thomas Beecham's opera company when on provincial tours. His uncle taught him to play the fiddle when he was very small, and even as a boy he was quite a proficient performer. The full advantage of this early start was felt when he was about fourteen, for the sudden death of his father made it necessary for him to start earning his own living forthwith. He was only fifteen when he was appointed a member of the Liverpool Philharmonic Orchestra, and within a year he achieved the further distinction of being admitted to the ranks of the Hallé Orchestra, thereby coming under the influence of the late Sir Hamilton Harty. He held these two appointments for ten years, during which he studied with Albert Sammons, and in due course rose to the position of deputy leader of the Hallé Orchestra. During this period four summers were spent abroad in taking further lessons from Carl Flesch.

In 1936 Matthews decided to try to specialize in solo work and accordingly resigned his orchestral appointments. He came to London and gave three excellent recitals at the Grotrian Hall, as a result of which he was offered a series of concerts in Finland. On this tour he made a significant impression in the Delius and Mozart concertos, which still occupy a prominent position in his repertoire.

On his return to England, Matthews gave a magnificent performance of the Elgar concerto with the Hallé Orchestra under Dr. Malcolm Sargent, thus inaugurating the association of his name with this monumental work. He has now played it well over thirty times in a manner that leaves one in no doubt about his admiration for it: he considers it to be the greatest modern violin concerto we possess. Many a music-lover will remember the astonishing performance he gave of it at the Coliseum with the London Philharmonic Orchestra in June 1941 : his seemingly effortless handling of its more difficult passages—and these are a gruelling test of any violinist—delighted everybody in the large audience.

The advent of war in 1939 was, of course, a great anxiety to all soloists who had to support themselves by means of their musical activity, and it is not surprising that Matthews accepted an invitation to return to the reconstructed Liverpool Philharmonic Orchestra as leader. Shortly afterwards, however, a similar invitation came from the London Philharmonic, and for one season he led both of these orchestras, but the strain proved too great, and in the following year he resigned his Liverpool appointment in order to devote all his time to the London Philharmonic Orchestra, and—naturally—to whatever solo work could be fitted in with their arrangements.

An important milestone in his career was the occasion in 1940 when he gave the first performance of Benjamin Britten's Violin Concerto with the London Philharmonic Orchestra under the direction of Basil Cameron. This is another extremely difficult work—one critic, it will be recalled, remarked that the composer had evidently made a point of exploring the very limits of human endeavour—but the fact that Matthews was invited to repeat it in the North of England and at Bristol with

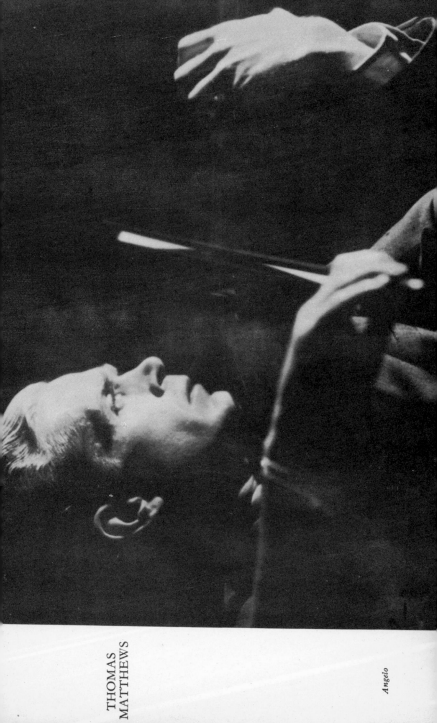

THOMAS MATTHEWS

Angelo

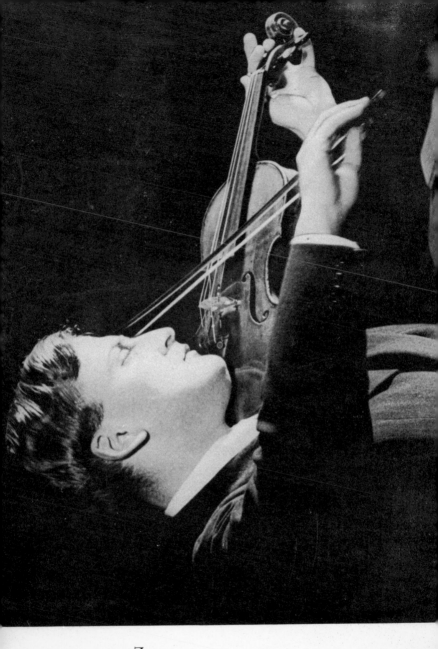

YEHUDI
MENUHIN

B.B.C.

the BBC Symphony Orchestra under Clarence Raybould, shortly afterwards, speaks for itself.

During the later years of the war, Matthews made several important tours of the Dominions, visiting New Zealand, Australia, South Africa and the Middle East. Among others, the concertos of Elgar, Britten, Beethoven, Delius, Brahms and Prokofiev were played to very large and appreciative audiences.

Another fine modern concerto with which the name of Thomas Matthews will be associated is that of William Walton. During 1946-7 he performed this outstanding work with the Hallé Orchestra under John Barbirolli no less than nine times. In the same year he was offered the head professorship of the violin at the Royal Manchester College of Music, an appointment which he still holds with a professorship at the Royal Academy of Music.

Matthews feels very strongly about the neglect of British artists for those of other countries by some of London's concert promoters. Ironically enough, British nationality appears to be an impediment to the success of an ambitious violinist only in English speaking countries, for Matthews himself has played as a guest soloist in Stockholm and Vienna, to mention but two cities of culture and discrimination from which he has received invitations. As an instance of this he has mentioned an occurrence in Johannesburg during one of his tours. A discriminating musician happened to overhear him playing over a few of the more difficult passages of a concerto in his room at an hotel, and went at once to the agent of a prominent impresario in a state of considerable excitement. "I have been listening to a remarkably brilliant violinist rehearsing at my hotel," he declared. "You ought to get into touch with him immediately and see if you can't fix up some concerts—he has wonderful possibilities."

"Have you discovered his name?" the agent asked eagerly.

H

"Yes. It's Matthews," the other replied.

The agent's face fell immediately, and he shook his head. "You can't promote a name like Matthews!"

The point that Matthews so often makes is that the English artist is so rarely given a fair chance of getting accustomed to concerto work. This is absolutely necessary if one is to rise to the height of such people as Heifetz or Milstein, both of whom he greatly admires. However brilliant he may be, a violinist cannot expect to give a beautifully polished performance of, say, the Beethoven concerto, if he never gets the chance of playing it with a symphony orchestra in public more than once a year. Practice at home, with the studying of gramophone records, is not the same.

Matthews uses a Matteo Gofriller, and prefers "Pirastro" strings—aluminium-covered. These, unfortunately, are extremely difficult to get at the present time. He always uses a Hill bow and considers this to be the finest make in the world. His pupils are allowed considerable latitude in the holding of the bow, though he invariably uses all four fingers on it himself. Similarly, he believes that fingering is a personal matter dictated largely by the shape of one's hand. Every violinist must himself determine the attitude of his left hand, avoiding movements that seem unnatural to him.

He thinks it is most essential that the violin student should learn the right way to practise early in life. So many work hard at the wrong sort of practice and do not discover the way to true progress until they have passed the "impressionable" years. The young violinist must learn to become his own critic: the average student does not listen enough to his own playing. A vitally important point to remember is that the tone of the violin you are playing sounds different to the right ear than to the left, owing to the fact that the latter is much nearer the instrument. It is the right ear that hears as the audience hear, yet the vast majority of violin students listen to their tone almost exclusively with the left—the right ear tends to become lazy because, consciously or unconsciously, the effort of listening is made by the left ear. This probably accounts for much of the bad intonation we hear to-day.

Another criticism that Matthews often makes is that there is too much uniformity in the playing of many violinists to-day. So few seem to be able to explore the amazing diversity of tone that the fiddle is capable of producing: they generally succeed in doing so only when they have become too old to give first-rate performances, for the gift of producing a large variety of tones is one that can come only with long experience. He considers that among his contemporaries Ginette Neveu is one of the few who are exceptionally gifted in this direction, and he urges young violinists to listen carefully to this artist's playing.

He advises the rising violinist to make a special effort to identify himself with a particular work, or a small number of works, or with a particular style of playing. Some—indeed many—say that this form of specialization is a disadvantage, but Matthews has come to the conclusion, from his own very considerable experience, that it is well worth while. So many of the really great works for the violin require such a tremendous amount of study if they are to be performed perfectly that it is better to rise to fame with a reputation for superb playing of two or three masterpieces than to remain in the ranks of mediocrity with a vast general repertoire. The standard of playing demanded to-day is extremely high, since audiences are becoming more and more discriminating every year, and of violinists in particular, they expect impeccable artistry.[1]

[1]An interesting point arises here. It is the author's opinion that before an average English audience a second-rate pianist can "get away" with a piano-smashing orgy in which every conceivable fault is apparent, yet the same audience will give only the mildest applause to a well-performed violin concerto. There is definitely a type of listener who honestly enjoys *any*

Matthews has always identified himself with the Elgar concerto, and no one will deny that he is one of the very few violinists in the world to-day who can give a really intelligent rendering of this masterpiece. His favourite concerto, incidentally, is the Brahms, which he believes to be the most wonderful work yet written for the violin, and one that demands the utmost skill in its execution.

Until a few years ago Matthews was a keen golf and tennis player, but he now finds that his time is wholly occupied with music. His love of chess, on the other hand, is undiminished. He considers it to be the greatest game in the world and confesses that he plays it at almost every meal-time!

type of violent piano-thumping provided that the destruction is carried out in the ritual of a concerto. Everybody knows that it is far more difficult to produce a beautiful sound from a violin than from a piano, yet virtuosity in a violinist is still relatively unappreciated by the majority of concert-goers. It requires something not far short of a miracle to make them applaud as heartily as they would for a splashy keyboard performance.

ISOLDE MENGES

ANOTHER eminent English violinist who in recent years has preferred to concentrate upon chamber music and teaching rather than concerto and other forms of solo work is Isolde Menges, whose youngest brother, Herbert, is the conductor.

Her father, George Menges, was of German descent, but married an Englishwoman, and between them they ran a successful school of music at Hove, where all their children were born. They spent their honeymoon in Germany and had dreams of having a child who would become a great violinist; in fact, with the rash optimism with which young musicians are apt to be endowed, they decided that while they were in Germany it would be well to buy the proposed child a suitable fiddle! So they acquired a good but tiny instrument and brought it home confident that it would be put to good use.

Thus Isolde Menges, their first-born, had greatness thrust upon her even before she was born. That event took place in the year 1893. It would have been too bad had she inherited none of her parents' musical gifts, but any anxiety they might have had about that was dispelled when she was quite an infant, for it soon became evident that she had a remarkable ear for music.

Before she reached the age of four she had given a little recital at her grandparents' house on the instrument her parents had acquired for her. Six pieces had been played entirely from memory, for she was unable to read music at that time, and had to learn everything by ear.

Isolde Menges received her early lessons from her father and mother in the company of her sister, Elfriede. Her two brothers, George and Herbert, were taught likewise, so all the four children grew up in an atmosphere of mutual music-making. Isolde even got the idea that everybody learned to play the fiddle as a matter of course, just as every child is taught to read and write, and was amazed when she visited some friends of the family one day and discovered people who could not do so.

A governess was engaged to take charge of her general education, and she was allowed to take additional music lessons with Leon Sammertini, who is now at the Chicago Conservatoire, and Emil Sauret. Then at sixteen, she went to Russia to study with Leopold Auer, and later spent two seasons with him at Dresden.

Her début was made at the Queen's Hall when she was about nineteen years of age. She played the Tchaikovsky concerto and the Lalo *Symphonie Espagnole* under the direction of Lyell-Taylor and was so successful that a further concert was arranged a fortnight later. At this she played the Beethoven and Wieniawski concertos. Her first recital took place on 14 March 1913 at the Bechstein Hall.

Three years later she embarked upon an extensive tour of America and Canada that lasted until 1919. This gave her the opportunity of appearing with such fine bodies as the Boston and Chicago symphony orchestras, and she was acclaimed by the American press as one of the greatest musical discoveries of the age. *Musical America*, for instance, said that she was by far the best female violinist that New York had ever known.

Those who imagine that concerts for schoolchildren are a recent innovation will be interested to know that during this tour Miss Menges gave well over a hundred concerts in various parts of Canada to audiences consisting exclusively of children, and gave patient explanations of all the music she played. She has always enjoyed introducing music to the young, and has a charming way of analysing it so that even the merest child can understand the composer's intentions.

During the nineteen-twenties Miss Menges toured all over Europe establishing an enviable reputation for herself, particularly in Germany where her playing has always been highly appreciated. Typical of the sort of notice she got is this report in *Der Reichsbote*:

"Isolde Menges' playing in the Blüthner Saal was so wonderfully musical, and showed such depth of feeling and beauty of tone that one at once recognized her as an artist of the first rank. Above all, she possesses the greatest essential, a strong artistic personality."

The famous Menges Quartet was founded in 1931 and originally consisted of Isolde Menges (first violin), Beatrice Carrelle (second violin), John Yewe Dyer (viola) and Ivor James ('cello). A few years ago Lorraine du Vall, a gifted Canadian violinist, replaced Miss Carrelle, and Jean Stewart took the place of John Dyer, though the latter still assists from time to time when quintets and sextets are performed.

Miss Menges became a professor at the Royal College of Music in 1931, and has never failed to find interest and satisfaction in teaching. To her pupils she passes on much of the wisdom she acquired from that world-famous master Leopold Auer: she still has vivid recollections of his remarkable classes, but she has no special "method", for no two pupils have hands exactly alike, and therefore it is useless to try to force upon them any set rules. Miss Menges emphasizes the significance of freedom of movement, and the student is always urged to "feel his way through the tone".

In bowing the importance of balance can scarcely be exaggerated: the third finger can be made to help the fourth a great deal in maintaining a good balance, while the significance of the thumb is not always realized. Moreover, students do not always understand that it is the first finger that has to give the tension.

Miss Menges deplores the modern method (favoured by some teachers) of concentrating exclusively upon technique at first, and then belatedly giving some attention to interpretation. She feels that if a student is to develop into a true artist he must learn technique and interpretation together. Interpretation is a vast subject: too vast to be mastered entirely in a lifetime, so every music student should start this part of his training at the earliest possible moment. Technique only enables him to reproduce what he wants: he must know *what* he wants from the start.

Too many young musicians have made a fetish of technique. They play the notes accurately but never seem to have asked themselves the question "What does the composer *mean* by this?" It is this unfortunate neglect of interpretation that accounts for the "dead" music we so often hear nowadays, and which is naïvely excused as "purist".

Although the student cannot do better than to work steadily at the classics it should be borne in mind that the works of the "virtuoso composers" are extremely useful in developing one's technique, and should be used regularly, even if one personally dislikes them.

Miss Menges' taste is conservative: she names Bach and Beethoven as the two "indispensable" composers, and if she were allowed to play the works of only two other composers she would choose Schubert and Mozart. Her "ideal" violinist is Heifetz, whose playing has always fascinated her, and she greatly admires that superb violist, William Primrose. There are, of course, various other fiddlers whose playing she enjoys, but mere musical acrobatics do not interest her.

Miss Menges was married in 1920 to Harold Tod Boyd, who wrote a fair amount of music for the violin. He died in 1946. Her son, David, is now a student at the Royal College of Music. He started learning to play the violin when he was very small on the same quarter-sized instrument that his grandparents had bought on their honeymoon—it is still in his mother's possession—but in time he showed a marked preference for the piano, and is now studying that instrument.

Isolde Menges uses a Guarnerius dated 1714, which —according to Hill—was made partly by Andrea Guarneri (circa 1626-1698) and partly by Guarneri del Gesù (1698-1744). She also possesses a fine Strad dated 1714.

Meeting her in her delightful home not far from Barnes Common, one begins to realize what a strong personality she is: every year of experience has added to her great store not only of musical knowledge but of understanding of the philosophy that lies behind the work of many of the greater composers. She reads theosophy, philosophy, and good fiction. Dickens and Thackeray are her favourites. But her accomplishments are not all intellectual: she is tremendously fond of her home and of animals (two cats, two dogs, a parrot and poultry!), and it is chiefly this domesticity that has, in recent years, made her less keen to tear about the world giving recitals.

YEHUDI MENUHIN

THE name of Yehudi Menuhin is almost a household word among those who are at all interested in music. He won the heart of the musical public as a child, and then did what comparatively few child prodigies succeed in doing when they grow up: he retained it. His boyhood triumphs made him one of the world's greatest box-office attractions, and although as an adult he has far more rivals than in former years, he can still be relied upon to draw a larger audience than most concert halls can accommodate.

He was born in New York on 22 April 1916, of Jewish parents. His father was born in Russia, but lived in Palestine for a while until he went to America as a teacher in a Jewish school in New York. Before Yehudi was a year old the little family moved to San Francisco, for his father had accepted an appointment there as head of a Hebrew educational organisation.

A story of his childhood tells us that when he was about three years old his unusual sensitivity to music induced a friend of the family to buy him a toy fiddle. Little Yehudi already considered himself to be too old for toys and scornfully refused to have anything to do with it. The friend then thrust it into his hands and asked him to play it "like a good little fellow". Whereupon Yehudi threw it angrily to the floor and stamped upon it.

This incident brought him a real violin on his fourth birthday, and Sigmund Anker was called in to give him lessons. No music pupil could have been more eager to

learn than little Yehudi, and within eighteen months
he was sufficiently advanced to go to Louis Persinger of
the San Francisco Symphony Orchestra. He never
seemed to weary of practising, and the progress he made
was such that, after playing in various private houses, he
was sought out to give public recitals. These were of
course minor affairs, but greater things were in store,
and he was only seven when he made his début with
the San Francisco Symphony Orchestra. An audience
of 9,000 gathered to hear him play the Mendelssohn
Concerto and were almost staggered by his amazing
skill.

As a result of this triumph he was invited to play
in New York, and appeared at the Manhattan Opera
House. His real début there, however, did not take
place until he was ten years old. Then he was given
the honour of playing the Beethoven Concerto at Carnegie
Hall with the New York Philharmonic Orchestra
conducted by Fritz Busch. On this occasion he used
not the twelve-dollar instrument that had been his
first love, but a three-quarter sized Grancino reputed
to be dated 1695 and worth over 10,000 dollars. Owing
to the smallness of his hands he was at that time unable
to tune it, and he had to pass it to the leader of the
orchestra two or three times for this purpose.

When the concerto started everybody's eyes were
trained upon the little boy in velvet breeches and white
shirt with short sleeves. He stood so quietly and
unconcerned during the *tutti* that many people—
including members of the orchestra—felt that he would
miss his entry. Surely this diminutive figure could not
match his skill with that of all these highly-trained
adult players? It seemed impossible. He would
probably continue to stand there and do nothing,
finally to run off the platform with a look of bewilder-
ment in his eyes. His entry came nearer and nearer,
and at the last moment—only a few bars before he was
due to start—he nonchalantly raised his fiddle and

started his gigantic task with all the self-assurance in the world.

It was a memorable occasion. He played like a virtuoso with thirty years' experience behind him. At the finish the audience found that mere clapping would not adequately express their feelings: cheer after cheer broke out, and several hundreds of the 3,000 present rose to their feet. Tears streamed from the eyes of old ladies, and after the first acknowledgment of the applause, Fritz Busch came down from his rostrum, took Yehudi in his arms and kissed him.

Olin Downes, the well-known American critic, said that he knew as soon as Yehudi's bow touched the strings that his performance would be an exceptionally intelligent one. Writing in the *New York Times* he reported:

"Menuhin has a technic that is not only brilliant but finely tempered. It is not a technic of tricks, but one much more solidly established, and governed by innate sensitiveness and taste. It seems ridiculous to say that he showed a mature conception of Beethoven's Concerto, but that is the fact. Few violinists of years and experience, known to the public, have played Beethoven with as true a feeling for his form and content, with such a healthy, noble, but unexaggerated sentiment, with such poetic feeling in the slow movement and unforced humor in the finale."

Menuhin's interpretation of the Beethoven Concerto was no doubt the result of his two years' study in Europe with Georges Enesco and Adolph Busch. He had also played in Paris with the Lamoureux Orchestra and gained some very valuable experience, so this enormous success in New York was not a surprise to many of his friends. At his Berlin début in 1929 he played both the Beethoven and the Brahms concertos with such feeling that many people said they had heard nothing like it since the days of Joachim. When

Yehudi walked off the platform he was met by Albert Einstein,[1] who said that his playing had proved to him that there was a God in Heaven.

His début in England took place shortly afterwards at the Queen's Hall, and this was followed by a recital in the Albert Hall. On both occasions his success was quite sensational.

A similar triumph took place on 14 November 1931 when at Leipzig Menuhin played with the famous Gewandhaus Orchestra at the great concert held to celebrate the 150th anniversary of its foundation. After the Mendelssohn Concerto, the conductor, Bruno Walter, described his playing as a miracle and said that the boy possessed genius of the highest order. This was the first time in the history of the Gewandhaus Orchestra that an encore was permitted: the audience were so persistent in their demand that they would not allow the programme to continue unless the "wonder boy" could play again. The concert was followed by a splendid banquet at which many of Germany's leading musicians, artists and scientists paid tribute to their young guest.

Some idea of the affection that was felt for Yehudi in musical and high social circles during his travels may be gained from the fact that when he was taken ill in Brussels, the late Queen Astrid commanded her own physicians to attend him, and cared for him as if he had been her own child.

For all that, the world's greatest conductor, Toscanini, would at one time have nothing to do with Menuhin. He heartily detested all child prodigies, having for years been pestered by ambitious parents, and would not consent to hear or even meet the lad. Adolph Busch tried again and again to persuade him to make an exception to his rule of ignoring all approaches from the representatives of child musicians,

[1]Not *Alfred* Einstein (the German musicologist) as some people believe.

and it took him over two years to convince the famous conductor that Menuhin was worthy of his attention. One day, Yehudi was rehearsing a concerto—quite a routine affair—and was taking no notice of the few odd people standing at the back of the hall. After all, at every rehearsal there are people connected with either the orchestra or the management of the hall who like to look in and see how things are going. He therefore made no special effort to impress them. To his astonishment, therefore, he had scarcely finished the last note of the concerto when he found himself taken up and kissed by an excited gentleman pouring forth superlatives in Italian. It was Toscanini: and from that day the *maestro* and the youthful artist have been the firmest of friends. Some time later, they went for a trip together and Toscanini had to listen to his young friend practising every day for hours on end. Those who know anything about the celebrated conductor's temperament will marvel at the fact that not a word of complaint came from him. When somebody asked him about it afterwards, Toscanini said that he had heard more good music on that trip than ever before in his life.

Another well-known little story about the two friends is of an occasion when Yehudi was playing the solo part of a Mozart concerto to him in private. Suddenly, the telephone bell rang. Toscanini immediately jumped up, tore it from the wall, and having silenced it for good by dragging out the wires, settled himself once again with the remark that now, perhaps, they could enjoy the music undisturbed.

Menuhin has, of course, been privileged to enjoy the acquaintance of many distinguished musicians, but one whose friendship he particularly treasured was Sir Edward Elgar. Yehudi was only fifteen when they first met: he had been asked to make a recording of the Elgar Violin Concerto and was anxious that the composer should hear his interpretation of it before undertaking this important commission. It was arranged that he should play it with piano accompaniment on a certain Saturday afternoon. He visited the great composer on the appointed day expecting to do anything up to ten or twelve hours' hard work, for he did not know that it took more than music to keep Elgar indoors on a beautiful summer's day. They started the concerto in the great man's study, but after the first page or two Elgar stopped them and said he was confident that the concerto would be all right in Menuhin's hands: it was such a lovely day, and the races were on. . . .

Shortly afterwards, Menuhin played this concerto under the composer's own direction: it was an experience he will never forget. Elgar seemed really inspired, and everybody played with a fervour that only the presence of a genius can engender. The concerto has been one of Menuhin's specialities ever since.

The young violinist was also a personal friend of the late Béla Bartók whose violin concerto he interpreted so perfectly that in 1944 the composer wrote his famous Sonata for unaccompanied violin expressly for him as a tribute. Menuhin gave the *première* of this at Carnegie Hall, New York, and later brought it to England to play it at one of his Albert Hall recitals.

We must now go back some years to mention the tours of Europe and the western half of America that Menuhin made during the years 1928-9. One of the most outstanding concerts of this period was when he played the Bach, Beethoven and Brahms concertos in a single evening with the Berlin Philharmonic Orchestra under Bruno Walter.

Those were years when his general education had also to be considered, and in order that he should have sufficient time for study and relaxation, Menuhin was allowed to accept no more than two public engagements a week. He generally averaged about fifty during a season.

It was in 1930 that his sister Hephzibah began to

appear with him. She was born at San Francisco in
1920 and is an accomplished pianist, a pupil of Marcel
Ciampi. Her début was made at the age of eight in
San Francisco, and although the general public knew
little of her before 1930, she had often accompanied
her brother at private recitals. A few years ago she
married Lindsay Nicholas, a young Australian farmer.
Menuhin has also a younger sister, Yaltah, who
frequently joins him in chamber music, being also a
fine musician. It is said that she has literary incli-
nations.

In 1935 Yehudi Menuhin made his first world tour,
visiting over sixty cities in over a dozen countries,
including Australia and New Zealand. Then he
withdrew from public life entirely for nearly two
years in order to study, to overhaul and vastly extend
his repertoire. Most of that period was spent on a
ranch in the Santa Cruz mountains, not far from Los
Gatos, California, a large and pleasant estate owned
by his parents.

When he reappeared, towards the end of 1937, and
made another world tour he was a mature artist in
every sense of the word: people spoke of him as one of
the greatest living masters of the violin. His studies
had convinced him of the value of several neglected
works, as, for instance, the so-called "Lost" Violin
Concerto in D minor of Schumann. This work,
especially, he included in several of his programmes,
thereby winning the approval of many of the critics.
The Strad[1] declared that he must be given the credit
for having "released that historically missing link
between the concertos of Beethoven and Brahms from
the library stacks to which the mysterious will of
Joachim had doomed it."

Again, it was Menuhin who discovered that Mozart
had specified the use of the mute in the second movement of his third concerto (G major).

[1]March, 1939.

In May 1938 he was married in London to Nola
Nicholas of Australia, sister of Lindsay Nicholas, who
was later to marry Hephzibah Menuhin. This marriage
was recently dissolved, and on Sunday 19 October 1947
he married Diana Gould, a ballerina, daughter of
Admiral Sir Cecil and Lady Harcourt, at Chelsea
Register Office while he was on a concert tour in
this country.

Menuhin is a robust young man, a picture of good
physique, and is keen on outdoor recreations. See him
riding in California and you would scarcely believe
that he was a professional musician. He loves camping
in the woods, swimming, cycling, walking and driving
his powerful car. Yet he is intellectually accomplished
as well: he can read and speak five languages, converse
upon art and politics, and hold his own in any company.
His literary taste reveals an unusually high standard
of intelligence.

To those who meet him for the first time he gives
the impression of being rather reserved. He is singularly
modest about his achievements and it is almost impossible to get him to talk about his successes in the concert
hall—in fact he does not discuss music to any great
extent except, perhaps, with Toscanini, who is still
his idol. Menuhin displays none of those silly signs of
"temperament" that some musicians believe to be
impressive; he is indeed a most placid young man and
never seems to worry about anything. Statistics from
the box-office mean nothing to him. His tastes are
simple, and the extravagance of some of the other
highly-paid musicians would appal him. This is perhaps
due to his careful upbringing; his parents never spoilt
him, despite the huge income he made, in fact his
father, who used to manage his affairs, is reported to
have said that Yehudi did not possess a current account
at the bank until he reached the age of twenty-
one.

J

During the Second World War Yehudi Menuhin made many tours in aid of war charities, some of them taking him as far afield as Australia. For the same cause he toured America in 1941 and crossed to England in 1943. In one year alone he made over 75,000 dollars for refugees.[1] He made an exciting tour of war areas in 1944 playing to the troops, and is proud to claim that he was the first artist to play in the Paris Opera House after the liberation of France. Recent performances in England have included an appearance at the Albert Hall on 26 June, 1945, when he played the Beethoven and the Bach E major concertos as well as the Vieuxtemps in D minor. The Beethoven and Bach were both played exquisitely, but the Vieuxtemps fell a little short of expectations, as did his performance of the Dvořák Concerto on 15 June 1946 (BBC Music Festival). At the Promenade concert on 27 August 1946 he won a great ovation although he was still not quite up to his usual standard. In the following year, however, his performances in this country were impeccable.

Menuhin can produce from his fiddle a tone unparalleled in the history of the violin: for cleanliness, smoothness and quality generally it is comparable with that of Heifetz, but is considerably warmer. His style is capable of seemingly innumerable variations, and technically difficult works simply do not worry him at all. The Bartók Concerto, which is considered to be one of the most difficult we possess, he plays with incredible ease.

His art is still developing, and he will not always interpret a work in exactly the same way. He was once told that he had played a Mozart sonata differently than on the previous occasion, and he at once admitted it, saying that his feeling for it had changed somewhat.

When preparing a work he goes over it several times, reading it mentally before he touches his fiddle, because he likes to listen to the sounds created by his

[1] It is reported that during the entire course of the War he raised well over five million dollars for various war charities.

imagination as his eye travels across the page. He always insists on playing from a first edition, and has some sharp things to say about editors who try to "improve" the classics. Toscanini and Enesco have been the most influential musicians in his conception of the works of the old masters, and he is always trying to repair the damage done to some of the more popular works by "clever" editors and those who are stupid enough to allow themselves to be misled by such vandals. He is not at all impressed by showy "virtuoso music", by the way, although he occasionally plays it in response to requests.

Among his collection of fiddles is the famous Khevenhueller Strad, which was not included in Hill's catalogue because it was in Russia for many years unknown to the connoisseurs. It was made over 200 years ago for Princess Khevenhueller of Austria and has been played by only four people since: Bohm, Joachim, Popoff and Menuhin, to whom it was given as a present for his twelfth birthday by one of his admirers in New York: Henry Goldman. It is worth over £20,000 to-day.

Menuhin's recordings are treasured by millions of violinists all over the world, and are used by hundreds of teachers in the instruction of budding soloists. Worthy of special mention are the Mozart Concerto No. 3 with the Orchestre Symphonique de Paris, the Dvořák Concerto in A minor made with the Orchestre des Concerts de la Société du Conservatoire, the Bach No. 1 in A minor, the E major and the Lalo *Symphonie Espagnole* with the Orchestre Symphonique de Paris, and the Mendelssohn Concerto with the Orchestre des Concerts Colonnes. All these were conducted by Georges Enesco.

Under Sir Malcolm Sargent, Menuhin recorded the Mozart Concerto in D major with the Liverpool Philharmonic Orchestra, but in this the solo part seems rather too restrained. Of special interest is his recording of the Elgar concerto under the composer's own direction with the London Symphony Orchestra; and both Menuhin and his master, Enesco, can be heard in the Bach Concerto in D minor for two violins made under the direction of Pierre Monteux. Menuhin has also recorded the Bruch Concerto No. 1 in G minor with the London Symphony Orchestra conducted by Sir Landon Ronald and the Paganini Concerto No. 1 in D with the Orchestre Symphonique de Paris under the direction of Monteux. The latter gives a good display of his fine technique, but his expression can be better appreciated in such a work (admittedly a minor one) as the Hebraic *Abodah* (Bloch), a recent recording.

NATHAN MILSTEIN

MILSTEIN was born on 31 December 1904 at Odessa, Russia, the birthplace of many of the world's greatest musicians, including two gifted pianists well known in this country.

As a boy he was keenly interested in music and did very well indeed with a local music teacher, Stoliarsky, during his schooldays. Deciding to make it his profession, he sought admission to the St. Petersburg Conservatoire, and was particularly gratified when he was given the honour of studying with two of the finest violinists of the day: Leopold Auer and Eugène Ysaÿe. The Great War was then in progress, but the effect of this was at the time less disastrous than that of the Revolution, for this drove most of Russia's leading musicians out of the country. Milstein, however, chose to remain, and the departure of the "great names" in music eventually proved to his advantage, for he was soon to seek public engagements.

Despite his undoubted talent, his early struggles were probably as arduous as those of any young artist of the present day—more so, in fact, for there were far fewer opportunities. Nevertheless, as soon as he left the Conservatoire he was able to get sufficient public engagements to maintain himself, so his professional career started forthwith.

Conditions in Russia were then appalling, and Milstein must have wondered on several occasions whether it was worth while going on. It was only the enthusiasm and gratitude of those music-lovers who were able to attend his concerts that made him persevere, though it is true that he was encouraged when in 1922 he met another brilliant young musician who was encountering the same difficulties. This was that amazing pianist Vladimir Horowitz, who was a few months older than Milstein and had just completed his course at the Kiev Conservatoire. The young violinist had been present at his début and had felt so convinced that Horowitz would rise quickly to fame that he suggested that they could perhaps tour together. Horowitz welcomed the idea, and they gave many concerts together, making a most favourable impression upon music-lovers wherever they went.

Because of difficulties in Russia, Milstein left that country in 1925 and proceeded first to Brussels where he sought instruction from Eugène Ysaÿe. But when this great master heard him play he said "There is nothing I can teach you that you do not know already", so the ambitious young violinist moved on to Paris. He arrived in the French capital unknown, with no money, very little music, and—worst of all—no fiddle. The only thing to do was to make as many contacts as possible and hope for the best. This unenviable task did bring him several new friends, however, and in time his great skill and deep devotion to music prevailed: one of his admirers offered to put up the money for a public concert, another offered to lend him a Strad, and thus he was able to make his début. Several critics were present at this concert and their favourable reports began to arouse considerable interest in musical circles. Various offers of further engagements came in during the ensuing weeks, including one from Spain, where he was immediately successful, and as Milstein became better known the demands for his services increased accordingly. Then came a tour of South America, and within two years he was recognized in half-a-dozen European countries as one of the rising violinists of the day.

It was undoubtedly his astonishing technique that brought him the honours in those days, for his interpretations were considered by some critics to be a trifle "raw". Fortunately, success never went to his head, and he was wise enough to learn from those who criticized his work intelligently. As a result, a few years on the concert platform made a world of difference to his style: his somewhat boisterous manner of playing became tempered, and although he will probably always be regarded as a violinist of the more vigorous type, he did, in those early days of public life, develop quickly into a very polished artist.

On his first visit to the United States in 1929, Milstein had the good fortune to meet Stokowski, who was immediately impressed by the young violinist's technique and arranged for him to make his American début with the Philadelphia Orchestra. Stokowski conducted, of course, and this great success put Milstein on his feet in the United States, the country in which he was to settle. He toured America and Canada every year until 1939, and became a naturalized American in 1943.

Milstein has never lacked admirers in Great Britain, and in more recent years, especially, we have come to regard him as one of the greatest of the celebrities who visit us from time to time. It is true that some people do not care for his style, but they are generally to be found among those who dislike the vigorous "school" of violinists. Milstein's playing would lose much of its character if he dissociated himself from this school of thought, and it would be a pity if he did so, for he enjoys spirited and strenuous music: it suits his technique. Many of his greatest successes have been in the performance of some of the most exacting works in the repertoire of the violin. He has played under almost every world-famous conductor, including Toscanini, Karl Muck, Bruno Walter, Furtwängler, Mengelberg and Beecham.

An interesting criticism of his playing is to be found in a report of one of his concerts made by a member of the *Musical Times* staff in the November 1936 issue of that august journal:

"To hear Nathan Milstein play eighteenth-century violin sonatas at his reappearance at Wigmore Hall on 22 October was to discover a new pleasure in chamber music. With Leopold Mittmann at the piano he gave Vivaldi's Sonata in A major with a fire and precision that fairly caught one's breath, just because it breathed life into music that until now had seemed to be dry bones. *This* was the Vivaldi whom Bach admired: not that pedagogue in whose likeness most people present the old Venetian. And when Milstein came to play Bach's own Sonata in G minor for violin and piano alone, he maintained the fire, adding to it dignity and tenderness. He has the strength, mental and physical, for this music, and a supple turn of speed that belongs to youth. One is accustomed by now to hearing fine technicians. Each has his special virtues. Milstein excels in the perfection of his playing of arpeggio passages of all kinds: his performance of the Presto in Bach's G minor was perfection itself. His Beethoven was less satisfying, not because anything was amiss with the execution but because some of Beethoven's thoughts —even in so open a sonata as the G major for violin and piano, Opus 30—are still to Milstein a closed book."

This criticism of Milstein's Beethoven might, perhaps, be disputed, but it is true that in the opinion of some of his admirers, his style is not particularly suited to certain works of this great composer. His interpretations are, on the whole, most enlightened, for he makes a profound study of all the music he plays, and of the lives of the composers concerned. Incidentally, he reads deeply on the other arts as well, and is quite a good painter in water-colours.

ISOLDE MENGES

NATHAN MILSTEIN

JEAN POUGNET

GINETTE NEVEU

His interpretation of the Brahms Concerto is always most satisfying, and gives one a very good idea of his musicianly qualities. This concerto was played by him at the Albert Hall during his visit to this country in 1947, and there must have been few in his large audience who were not thrilled by his intensely sincere and accurate rendering which, one felt, brought out all the grandeur and nobility of this famous concerto.

Other concertos in his repertoire of which he is particularly fond are the Mozart, Mendelssohn, Tchaikovsky, Glazounov and Dvořák. In his recital programmes he invariably includes an unaccompanied Bach Partita and frequently two or more of the Paganini Caprices, besides sonatas of Beethoven, Brahms, Prokofiev, etc.

One of the recent additions to his extensive repertoire has been the Stravinsky Concerto, of which he gave a truly remarkable performance in New York with the Philadelphia Orchestra under Ormandy a few years ago.

During the Second World War, Milstein served as Chairman of the National Committee of Concert Artists for the U.S. Treasury's War Bond Campaign, and spent much of his time in giving recitals in support of the campaign.

In private life, he is a rich personality, well read and keenly interested in many outdoor activities. He loves walking, climbing, swimming, motoring and even cycling. Switzerland is a country that never fails in its appeal to him, and he always tries to visit it during the summer—if possible with his very old friend Horowitz. He plays a good game of both lawn and table tennis.

For many years, Milstein played the "Dancla" Strad, but in 1944 he acquired the famous "Monasterio" Strad. The latter was used by him in public for the first time to celebrate the Allied Victory. Towards the

end of 1946 he bought yet another Strad, the so-called
"Ex-Goldmann" (dated 1716), which was hidden in
Europe throughout the Second World War, and which
he has renamed the "Maria Thérèse", after the names
of his wife and daughter. According to Hill, it is one
of the finest Strads in existence. Milstein generally
uses a Tourte bow, of which he has several excellent
specimens.

GINETTE NEVEU

GINETTE NEVEU'S sweeping successes during her earlier visits to England are still vivid in the memories of thousands of music lovers: everybody liked this unassuming French girl, and it was difficult to restrain one's use of superlatives when describing her genius for interpretation, for it was this rather than her impeccable technique that put her in the front rank of contemporary violinists. Fine technicians, after all, are less of a rarity these days, but it is seldom that one finds a young violinist with so marked a gift for getting to the very soul of the music—for understanding the emotions that caused the composer to put pen to paper. Soon after her triumphs in England, Ginette Neveu embarked upon an extensive tour of America, and the reception that she is getting there as this book goes to press is further proof that she is destined to become one of the few really great violinists of the century.

She was born in Paris on 11 August 1919 and was blessed with a musical environment from the beginning of her life. Her mother, who was her first teacher, was a well-known violinist and professor of music, while her father, though only an amateur, was sufficiently accomplished on the fiddle to take part in all the music-making that went on at home. And here we must also make the acquaintance of her talented brother, Jean, who was later to become an excellent pianist and his sister's favourite accompanist.

Ginette Neveu began her study of the violin at the age of five, and taking her music very seriously, made astonishing progress. She was little more than seven when she had the honour of appearing in the great amphitheatre of the Sorbonne with the Colonne Orchestra under the direction of Gabriel Pierné.

She continued her studies, and a few years later went to the Paris Conservatoire, where for twelve months she worked under Jules Boucherit. After that, she became a pupil of the late Carl Flesch, for whom she had the greatest admiration.

It was before the end of the Second World War— immediately after the liberation of Paris—that she first came to England : a comparatively unknown French girl who had never before played outside her native land. With the French conductor, Roger Desormieres, she made a fairly extensive tour of this country and became such a favourite artist that she was asked to make no fewer than eight return visits during the ensuing year or two. With her brother Jean, she gave a large number of recitals and also appeared at many orchestral concerts under such conductors as Sir Adrian Boult, Sir Malcolm Sargent, Walter Süsskind, Basil Cameron, Charles Münch and Issay Dobrowen. "England is a wonderful country for music," she declares, "and in this art she is leading the world. I have been very happy to meet a great number of your young artists, and I believe that England has some very great composers at the present time—William Walton and Benjamin Britten especially. I have been particularly impressed by the fact that your audiences are not only cultivated from the classical point of view but are genuinely anxious to hear new works and to understand new tendencies in music. The English orchestras, particularly the BBC Symphony Orchestra, the Hallé, and the London Philharmonic, are among the finest in the world, and your recordings are the most perfect I have heard.

"Not only do I owe the English my deepest gratitude for having been the first to invite me to a foreign country, but I consider that music now holds such an important position in England that no artist could establish an international reputation without having appeared in your fine country."

Ginette Neveu has now enjoyed great successes in several other countries, her most important appearances, up to the time of writing, having been in Vienna (with the Philharmonique), Copenhagen (Staatsradiofonien), Stockholm and Amsterdam (Concertgebouw), Boston (with the Boston Symphony Orchestra under Serge Koussevitzky) and New York (with the Philharmonic-Symphony Orchestra conducted by Charles Münch.) She has, of course, also played several times in Paris with the Société des Concerts du Conservatoire.

She frequently gives sonata recitals with her brother Jean, who studied the piano at the Paris Conservatoire under the eminent Yves Nat, and who invariably acts as her accompanist when she plays purely solo works. Her preferences in music, by the way, are for Bach, Brahms and Beethoven, but she also makes a very conscientious study of contemporary music. Her fiddle is a lovely Stradivarius dated 1730, and she always uses Pirastro strings.

Her principles in music she summarizes thus : "*L'art d'un artiste est de toujours créer les oeuvres maîtresses de la littérature musicale et l'instrument dont il se sert n'est qu'un moyen d'accéder à ce but.*"

She is interested in literature, painting, social problems and, generally speaking, all that represents a spiritual life in this world. To her, the other arts are not merely recreations in the popular sense of the word, for in her life "everything is recreation."

At the time of writing, many of the best recordings she has made in this country have yet to be issued, but of those now available, her fine recording of the Sibelius Concerto in D minor made with Walter Süsskind and the Philharmonia Orchestra is the most important, though there is splendid playing in some of the smaller pieces, notably the *Danse Espagnole* of Manuel de Falla, the *Hora Staccato* by the Roumanian composer Dinicu, and the *Four Pieces* by the late Josef Suk.

Ginette Neveu has made many friends in this country, all of whom have testified to her warm-heartedness and delightful sense of humour. She is quite without affectation, and makes no show of what some people fondly imagine to be "artistic temperament". She has a strongly marked personality which does not, however, obscure that of the composers whose work she plays.

NOTE. As the second impression of this book was in the hands of the printers, news was received of the sudden death of Ginette Neveu and her brother Jean in an air crash on San Miguel Island in the Azores early on Friday, 28th October, 1949. When her body was found it was observed that her Stradivarius —her most precious possession—was clutched tightly in her arms. The violin, though broken, had not been burned.

JEAN POUGNET

MOST people seem to be under the impression that Jean Pougnet is a Frenchman; indeed it has been stated several times that he was born in Paris, but this is quite incorrect. He is of French ancestry, it is true, and speaks the language perfectly, but even his parents were British subjects; in fact his father held a civil service appointment on the island of Mauritius, where Jean was born in 1907. His father was an excellent pianist, by the way, and frequently gave lessons to local residents aspiring to play that instrument.

The family moved to this country when Jean was two years of age. His aptitude for music was discovered by his sister Marcelle, who gave him his first lessons on the violin when he was about seven, and his general interest in the art was no doubt encouraged by the activities of his brother René, an able pianist.

It so happened that they lived opposite that eminent teacher Rowsby Woof, and because Jean seemed unusually promising his sister took him across to their neighbour and asked if anything could be done for the boy. Woof was certainly impressed by Jean's playing and accepted him as a private pupil. In due course—when he was eleven—he won a scholarship to the Royal Academy of Music, where he studied for the next seven years.

Jean Pougnet's first public appearance was when he was in his twelfth year: he played a variety of pieces at the King's Hall, Covent Garden. But of far greater importance, of course, was the recital he gave at the

Wigmore Hall just before his sixteenth birthday: this was a great success artistically, and led to his appearance, shortly afterwards, at a Promenade concert.

While he was at the Academy, Pougnet had an excellent quartet and did an extensive amount of chamber music as well as occasional solo performances. But he finished his academic training at a time when it was far from easy for a young musician to make a living exclusively in "straight" music, and for the first few years of his career he had the moral courage to pocket his pride and earn honest guineas by doing solo work for a few of the leading dance bands. It should be emphasized here that Pougnet is no snob: he has always enjoyed good dance music, and is absolutely sincere in his belief that the better class of dance band serves a useful purpose both socially and artistically. Few people realize what a high standard of musicianship is possessed by some of the better type of dance musicians. During this period of his career he was building up a considerable classical repertoire, and frequently gave recitals at the Wigmore Hall.

As soon as he felt sufficiently well established in "straight" music, Pougnet abandoned his work for the dance bands and undertook a variety of engagements: solo recitals, concertos, chamber music, broadcasts, recordings, and even went as far afield as the film studios to make recordings for screen productions. His broadcast trios with William Primrose and Anthony Pini were particularly good.

At the outbreak of the Second World War he was chosen to lead that very select little band of players known as the BBC Salon Orchestra; a fine ensemble that did excellent work until its dissolution later in the war years. Then, in 1942, he accepted an appointment that was to make him a familiar and greatly admired figure in every concert hall in the country: the leader-ship of the London Philharmonic Orchestra. From that time until the fall of Germany he led this stout-hearted body of players through all the vicissitudes of those difficult years. The story of their experiences as they went up and down the country taking music and cheer to war-weary civilians and service people has been told elsewhere[1].

In December 1945, Jean Pougnet bade farewell to his colleagues and embarked upon a career as a soloist. He had for some time been experiencing an increasing demand for his solo services, and as the building up of a virtuoso's repertoire these days is a formidable task, he felt compelled to make a clean break so that the whole of his time could be devoted to solo work. He still retains his interest in chamber music, of course, and it is to be hoped that we shall still hear him quite frequently in small ensembles.

Pougnet is undoubtedly one of the most brilliant of the younger school of violinists and unless we encounter another of those musical slumps that play havoc among the lives of musicians, he would appear to have a fairly easy road to fame. Technical difficulties do not seem to perplex him at all—notice how easily he sweeps through the extremely difficult last movement of the Delius concerto—and his style has a refinement that the more discriminating type of listener is bound to appreciate. It is quite an individual style: light, fastidious and restrained, and very pleasant in a wide range of works. Moreover, he has a reputation for accuracy and possesses a good sense of rhythm.

Of his recordings the best are perhaps the Bach Double Concerto for two violins, made with Arthur Grumiaux and the Philharmonia String Orchestra conducted by Walter Süsskind with Dr. Boris Ord of King's College, Cambridge, at the harpsichord; and his fine recording of the Delius Concerto made with

[1]Briefly in my *Conductors' Gallery*, and in more detail in the interesting publications of the Orchestra's able secretary, Mr. Thomas Russell.

K

the new Royal Philharmonic Orchestra under Sir Thomas Beecham. The former was made for Columbia; the latter for H.M.V. under the auspices of the Delius Trust. But because of its considerable merit mention must also be made of the Trio in G by E. J. Moeran (recorded with Frederick Riddle, viola, and Anthony Pini, 'cello).

Pougnet is an "idealist to the last degree" to quote his own words, and has no narrow-minded prejudices concerning music. He is interested in everything that is worth playing and is a keen student of modern music. He made a very good impression a year or so ago at a Covent Garden concert in the Bloch concerto, for instance, and recently gave the first English performance of a concerto by Richard Arnell. At the time of writing, two of our contemporary composers are engaged upon works that will be dedicated to him.

In person, he is very pleasant, and modest in the extreme. He dislikes talking about himself and even tends to under-estimate the value of the great experience he gained as an orchestral player. He is rarely to be seen in London unless he has a definite engagement, for his spare time is generally spent in study or recreation at his home on the Sussex coast. He was married in 1929 to Frances Lois, a Londoner, and has no children; the third member of the little family being an immensely lovable Great Dane, to which both Jean and his wife are quite devoted.

When Pougnet requires some diversion from his fiddle—a very fine Januarus Gagliano, by the way— he generally turns to something mechanical. He is clever at contriving all manner of gadgets and is a most useful "man about the house". He never seems to worry about his hands, and if you were to pay him an unexpected visit you would probably find him working hard in his garden or sawing up the branches of a recently-lopped tree. On the platform he is apt to give the impression of being a very fastidious young man, but at home he is as unassuming and domesticated as any suburban husband.

TO those who are interested in the art of violin playing, the name of Max Rostal means more than that of a virtuoso: it is a name associated with what one might describe as a "movement" in the art, for the ideas— and ideals—of this enlightened artist are being carried into the world of music by an ever-increasing circle of musicians who either were, or still are, his enthusiastic students.

Max Rostal was born in Austria in 1905 and started to play the violin at the age of five. A year later he gave his first public concert, which was the beginning of a career as an infant prodigy. He toured a large number of towns in Central Europe and frequently had the honour of playing at the Austrian Court.

His first serious course of study was with Professor Rosé in Vienna, but at the age of thirteen he went to Carl Flesch. Four years with this master enabled him to make his début as an adult musician at the age of seventeen and he was then given plenty of opportunities of touring in most European countries. He was only about twenty when he won the Mendelssohn Prize at the International Competition held in Berlin.

Even in those early days he was keenly interested in teaching and readily accepted an invitation to become the official assistant to Carl Flesch in Berlin. This appointment he held until he was nominated to a professorship at the State Academy of Music in Berlin in 1929. As far as his official duties permitted he continued to give regular concerts and he was able to undertake several tours.

He bitterly resented the Nazi Party's intervention in cultural affairs and early in 1934 found himself dismissed from office in the company of many other distinguished musicians, including Schnabel, Hindemith and Feuermann. As he had several friends in England he came to London with a number of his pupils, determined to start afresh, and in time succeeded in establishing himself, though not without some difficulty, of course. He found us very reserved at first, but he soon got to understand our mentality and has since been acclaimed enthusiastically by audiences and friends alike. Of the British audiences he is especially appreciative: he delights in the faithfulness they show to all good musicians.

Since his arrival in this country he has played with all the leading symphony orchestras and done a great deal of broadcasting. His recording of the complete set of Beethoven violin sonatas for Decca is yet another of his outstanding undertakings. He continued to live in London throughout the air raids and the flying bomb and rocket attacks, and also visited many of the provincial cities suffering from aerial bombardment to give recitals and concerts. It will perhaps be recalled that on Derby station one Saturday evening during the blackout he fell over a mailbag when running for a train and broke a rib.[1] This put him out of action for four weeks.

His teaching remains an important part of his activity and it is appropriate that he has been appointed a Professor and Fellow of the Guildhall School of Music. A much wider field of opportunity, however, has recently been opened to him by the invitation he has received from the BBC to give talks in the series "Studies in Interpretation and Style" in the Third Programme, and many a musician who might never have the opportunity of studying with him in London has been able to learn something of his ideas.

[1] Not a *wrist* as several newspapers reported.

Another interesting branch of Max Rostal's activity is the editing and arranging of music, and research work on seventeenth and eighteenth century music. It was while he was thus engaged that he discovered the manuscript of a work by Tartini that had never been published. This he was able to arrange for publication (Novello), after which he gave the first performance of it.

Rostal has never been very happy about using the existing *cadenzas* in the Beethoven concerto, and it occurred to him some time ago when he was looking through Beethoven's unfortunate piano arrangement of the work that he could transcribe for violin the *cadenzas* which the composer had added for the piano version. This he did, and the result was most gratifying. These *cadenzas* were then published by Boosey & Hawkes, so it is now possible for any violinist to play the concerto with *cadenzas* written by Beethoven himself. Rostal invariably plays them whenever he performs this concerto in public.

In the music of his contemporaries, Max Rostal takes the keenest interest, and he has had the honour of performing many English works for the first time. These include the concerto by Bernard Stevens, Benjamin Frankel's Sonata for violin, the *Meditation* and *Lyric Interlude* by Alan Bush, the sonatina by Robin Orr, as well as that of Lennox Berkeley, and many other works. In his extensive repertoire the concertos of Moeran, Bax and Bartók figure prominently, and his name will always be associated with that remarkable concerto by the Soviet composer Khachaturian, of which he gave the first performance in this country.

To give even a rough outline of all Max Rostal's ideas on violin playing would be impossible here, but he has certain strong points of view that must be understood if one is to appreciate his approach to the art.

He insists, for instance, that a violinist must be

acquainted with the life of the composer he is trying to interpret, and with the social background of his period. It is impossible for any instrumentalist to translate into sound all the emotions, thoughts and peculiarities of the composer if he is entirely ignorant of his life, his temperament, beliefs, struggles, social environment and so forth. Moreover, no violinist can properly interpret a work if he is familiar with the composer's violin music only. Rostal declares, for example, that a violinist cannot comprehend Bach unless he understands the great emotional experience that is the very soul of such works as the *St. Matthew Passion* or the B minor Mass. Similarly, how can one play even a minor work of Beethoven intelligently unless one understands the symphonies and string quartets and knows something of the thoughts of the composer?

Max Rostal is equally outspoken about the type of violinist who learns the solo part of a concerto and then calmly includes the work in his repertoire without even bothering to study the full score. It is unfortunately true that there are violinists who know nothing more of the orchestral part than their entries, and even these have more often than not been learned from a piano edition. How can one play the solo part of a concerto with understanding when one is entirely ignorant of the form or "structure" of the work as a whole? We are told that more than one soloist has discovered with some surprise during a concerto that the orchestra was playing and developing the principal theme!

The necessity of a proper understanding of the composers, and of their major works, is continually being impressed upon Rostal's pupils. "The richer the mind, the richer the experience, the more colourful your interpretations will be," he declares. "You can't have too much technique, but technique alone is of no interest if the emotional and spiritual side is neglected."

Max Rostal believes that the shallow-mindedness of some violinists was partly responsible for the decline in the interest of violin concertos and solos generally a few years ago. The violinist should always remember that owing to the very nature of his instrument he must maintain a higher standard than the average pianist: he has far less chance of "getting away" with a slovenly performance. As Max Rostal neatly puts it: "The violin has no pedal!"

His pupils are also urged to distrust the markings of editors and to seek as far as possible (in manuscripts, first editions, etc.) the composer's own indications on every work that is studied. Even the rhythm and notes of men's works have sometimes been altered by conceited editors, and the true musician must be willing to go to endless trouble to rectify vandalism of this type. "The majority of editions are not to be trusted," Rostal declares.

The question of style in playing is one that has always been a matter of great concern to this artist. Too much attention has already been paid to the "style" of individual violinists and their adherents, and this has been the cause of a great deal of wrong thinking. Strictly speaking, the violinist should have no personal style at all (if such a thing exists), because the style should always be that of the composer he is interpreting at the time. The so-called "Golden Tone" associated with Kreisler has been made almost ridiculous by indiscriminate use: it is, as Rostal says, like pouring golden syrup over everything you eat, including fish, meat and vegetables! Every single work requires its own peculiar type of expression: there are, of course, many similarities, but it is useless to try to prescribe any definite style or tone for any particular composer. Even within a single work, different types of expression and tone are frequently called for. "Golden rules" and generalizations are not only inartistic but definitely misleading. The solution, surely, is for the musician to become a faithful artist by making a sincere study of everything he performs.

This brings us to another point: the extremists in the opposite direction who, with the fond belief that they are siding with the "purists", have evolved a non-emotional style of playing that throws overboard all the good traditions of the art, and with it, most of the knowledge that has been gained from the masters. The result is a cold, chromium-plated type of playing that has little but a pseudo-modernism to recommend it.

It has been said by some that Max Rostal is establishing an English "school" of violin-playing, for none exists at the present time, but it is doubtful whether he would make such a claim himself, knowing the prejudice that this might cause in certain quarters. Nevertheless, his influence in this country is of the utmost significance to the art of violin-playing, for he has pupils, or ex-pupils, in every symphony orchestra of any importance in England, as well as those who spread the good news by teaching his methods, or are making a name as soloists and chamber-music players. Students come to him from all parts of the world: at the present time, for instance, America, South Africa, Australia, New Zealand, Palestine, Sweden and Switzerland are represented among his pupils. Time may prove that just as one of our most famous orchestras was founded by a German, what may prove to be one of the most important schools of thought in English violin-playing will owe its existence to an Austrian, who, incidentally, became a naturalised British subject soon after the end of the Second World War.

A few years ago Max Rostal acquired a superb Strad dated 1697, which is now known as the "Rostal Strad", since it possessed no other designation. He previously used a Guarnerius. His A and D strings are aluminium-covered; his G and E being the usual silver-covered and steel respectively, and he prefers to use modern bows.

In private life, Max Rostal is a man of many interests, though he would always say that music is his principal hobby, and that he is one of those fortunate people whose work is also their recreation. He is a keen collector of first editions of music, not merely because of an acquisitive instinct but because first editions are less likely to bear the marks of "clever" editors.

In art his interest is centred around the work of the French Impressionists, and he has several excellent examples of their works upon his walls. His reading, apart from books on music, is chiefly of philosophical works, but he frankly admits that he can often be caught with one of the better types of thriller, his taste for this sort of literature having been acquired chiefly in railway carriages when something fairly light, yet entirely absorbing, was necessary to while away the many weary hours of travelling that it has been his misfortune to endure.

Out of doors his chief recreation is the driving of his powerful car, and he is never more pleased than when he is able to indulge in a few weeks' motoring in Switzerland. He is also very fond of animals—cats and dogs in particular.

A visit to his house in Hampstead would make any music-lover envious, not only of his fine library, but of a delightful detached music studio of the type that most of us long for, but so rarely succeed in acquiring (to the disappointment not only of ourselves but of our unfortunate neighbours). This one, at the end of his garden, which, by the way, suggests that he has a positive distaste for lawn-mowing, is a light and spacious sound-proof affair that houses his collection of instruments, including a fine grand piano, and his patiently collected library of scores—some thousands of them. There is a no-nonsense atmosphere about this musician's workshop, and one cannot help feeling a little sympathetic towards the students who have to stand there and have their work criticized by this very shrewd artist. However, Max

Rostal radiates an air of confidence, and one feels that after a year or two in this studio with him one could face an audience consisting of nothing but Richard Capells and Ernest Newmans without turning a hair.

ALBERT SAMMONS

THERE must surely be few executive musicians of to-day who have done more in the cause of English music than Albert Sammons, and it was with great pleasure and satisfaction that the musical world heard of his award of the C.B.E. in the Birthday Honours of 1944. With all due respect to the great virtuosi of other nations, there is something refreshingly different about the playing of "our own Albert", as one conductor has referred to him, and if one may be forgiven a somewhat extravagant analogy, it is rather like going for a brisk walk across Wimbledon Common on a breezy spring morning after an hour spent in the humid atmosphere of a greenhouse in Kew Gardens. There is beauty, plenty of it, in both cases, but in the former there is physical stimulation as well, and in this country most of us find that a very agreeable mixture. This does not mean that foreign violinists are incapable of giving a stimulating performance, because there are half-a-dozen at least who pride themselves upon their unusual ability to stir their audiences in this way, but the stimulating qualities in the art of Albert Sammons are characteristically English, and to define them precisely here would be as impossible as an attempt to analyse somebody's personality in a couple of hundred words. And how immeasurably more difficult it is to dissect the art of the executive musician than that of the composer, the painter, sculptor or writer, for no two performances are exactly alike. But surely, the reader will ask, the gramophone gives the violinist's art a degree of permanence? That is true, but can one really judge a man's art from a mechanical reproduction of it? Here we come to a very controversial point over which a great deal of concern is felt. It is now quite an old topic, so little more need be said here, except that it is a matter that will crop up again later in this chapter.

No, one can do little more than to say that the outstanding feature of Albert Sammon's playing, and that which appeals so strongly to us in this country, is its reflection of the wholesome qualities that go towards the making of what we are still proud to call the English way of life: its integrity, sturdiness, cleanliness, its lack of affectation and that horrible, morbid trait that some musicians cultivate with the notion that it is an essential attribute of genius. This style is built upon the sure foundation of excellent technique and a sincere desire to play faithfully the music he loves.

As a man, he is the most normal person imaginable. In town he would pass for a stolid business man with a substantial house in one of the better-class suburbs; in the country he might easily be mistaken for the principal solicitor in the local market town with a grim determination to buy all the best of Sir John's silver as soon as the income tax collector succeeds in driving the poor old boy into his grave. But meet him in London and discuss music with him, and you begin to realize that here is an unusually knowledgeable musician who has derived the utmost benefit from his many years' experience as an orchestral player, in chamber music and as a soloist. That is an important point, for Albert Sammons has never been too proud to learn, in fact he readily acknowledges that he is almost entirely self-taught. How different has been his career from that of the pampered virtuoso whose complacency sets in at an early age and stifles all further artistic progress, who establishes a repertoire in his 'teens and then drags it all over the world for the rest of his life like a conjuror with a bag of tricks. Sammons is of the type who realizes that a true musician never stops learning; a musician's education is never complete.

Yet it is not until he takes up his fiddle to illustrate some point that he altogether ceases to be the conventional type of man that his appearance suggests. An expression of deep concentration and sensitivity appears on his face, and if you watch him carefully as he calmly plays a dozen bars of some extremely difficult concerto you realize that he listens with the utmost care to every note he produces. Watch his eyes, and you will see that every note, every phrase, every expression, is subjected, as it were, to an acid test as soon as it is created. He has an exceptionally acute ear, and this undoubtedly accounts for much of the merit in his playing.

The life of Albert Sammons has not been an easy one. He had the advantage of neither silver spoon nor wealthy patron in his early days; he has climbed the ladder rung by rung, from the very bottom to the very top. He was born in London on 23 February 1886, and in his childhood was encouraged to take an interest in music by his father, who was a good amateur violinist. No lad could have worked harder to master the fiddle than Albert Sammons, and as his parents were not wealthy, he soon began to look around for opportunities to earn his own pocket money with his beloved instrument. One thing led to another, and when this enterprising boy was about eleven years old he received an engagement to play every evening in a Piccadilly restaurant. The idea of a boy of that age earning his own living seems almost fantastic to us to-day, but it certainly did him no harm. He was blessed with good physique, and never complained of the strain of playing for several hours every evening after tiring days at school. The orchestra played a wide range of light classical music, and the experience was, of course, of the utmost value; indeed, when Albert left school at the age of twelve, he had no difficulty in securing an engagement to play three times a day in the Earl's Court Exhibition orchestra. Looking back, he realizes that much was accomplished in those early days: restaurant orchestras and the like were good training grounds for any young musician, since they invariably played tolerably good music, including operatic selections. The jazz band of to-day is a poor substitute and offers very little scope to the music student who is obliged to earn his living.

So Sammons continued to educate himself, though it is true that he took half-a-dozen lessons or so from F. Weist-Hill and John Saunders. His periods of study had to be fitted in between all manner of engagements, in the orchestras of theatres and hotels, and in various other ensembles, some of which were formed for playing at balls and other social functions. Many a time did he don elaborate "musical comedy" uniforms for the purpose of playing in Hungarian bands and suchlike. He often recalls with a chuckle one Hungarian band in which he frequently played: it was supposed to be a genuine ensemble from Central Europe, and the players were strictly forbidden to talk in case it was discovered that very few, if any, could speak anything but English— and that with a pronounced Cockney accent! Like most other English musicians, Sammons learnt at an early age that English nationality was the greatest obstacle in the musical career of those who aspired to rise from the ranks of the orchestra. But he steadfastly refused to change his name, as several of his colleagues had done, to something ending in "ini" or "etti" or "ski" or "berg". Several people suggested that if he had a year or two abroad and then returned with an imposing foreign name and, perhaps, a habit of speaking in broken English, he might rise quickly to fame, for his remarkable technique was already the subject of comment. It was a great temptation, but he decided that it was his duty to play his part in breaking down the absurd prejudice against the English musician, so he would hear no more about it.

He continued his struggle, earning his living as a rank-and-file musician, studying in his spare time, earning a few honest guineas here and there by teaching, and consoling himself that sooner or later his "break" would come. Many a time did he miss the last horse-drawn 'bus and have to walk home three or four miles while some foreign musician of lesser skill was being taken back to one of London's more exclusive hotels in a carriage.

At last, after some six or seven years, his opportunity came. One evening in 1908 he played the last two movements from the Mendelssohn Concerto at the Waldorf Hotel, and was quite unaware that anybody of musical importance was listening to him. Much to his surprise Sir (then Mr.) Thomas Beecham came forward to congratulate him, and later offered him the leadership of an orchestra he was forming in connection with a new venture in operatic and symphonic work. Sammons accepted on the spot, and held this post for the next five years, during which his progress was quite remarkable.

Like most other good students of the violin, he had a deep love of chamber music. Nothing pleased him more, therefore, than the offer he received in 1909 to become the first violin of that able group of musicians later known as the London String Quartet. Warwick Evans, Waldo Warner and Thomas Petre were the other members. With them he toured Europe and proved to foreign audiences that England could produce string players comparable with any that came from the Continent. This association lasted until 1919, the year in which Sammons decided to give up string quartet work so that he could specialize as a soloist. This did not mean that he had lost any of his love for chamber music: far from it.

His first concerto engagement was at the Kursaal

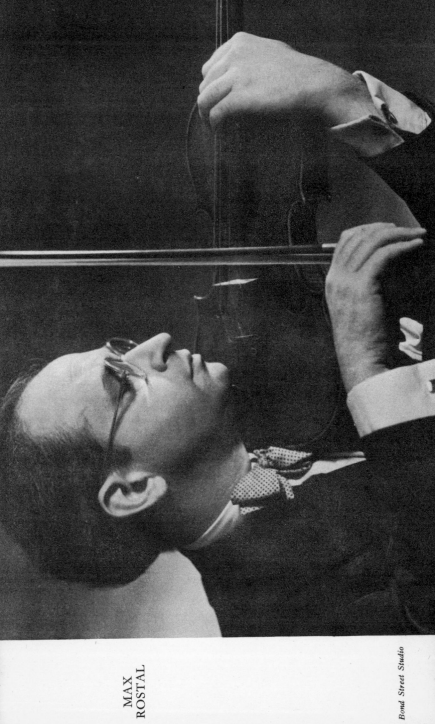

MAX
ROSTAL

Bond Street Studio

ALBERT
SAMMONS

Hay Wrightson

at Harrogate, but he was "discovered" as a soloist when he played the G minor Concerto by Max Bruch at the Queen's Hall under Stanford. Imagine his joy when a day or two later he received a letter from Sir Landon Ronald saying that he had never heard a finer performance and inviting him to play at the Albert Hall.

Perhaps one of his most treasured memories of those early days, however, was the occasion in 1912 when he had the honour of playing the Saint-Saëns B minor Concerto before King George V and Queen Mary, and in the presence of the composer. He had been appointed Musician in Ordinary to His Majesty in the previous year.

It is significant that Sir Thomas Beecham has always held the opinion that Albert Sammons has at all times fully justified his early confidence in him. Through his connection with the great conductor, Sammons received many excellent appointments, including the leadership of the Royal Philharmonic Society orchestra. He also went to Berlin as leader of Beecham's Russian Ballet orchestra, and toured the British Isles with that conductor's own symphony orchestra.

In 1913, Sammons accepted an appointment as leader of the Dieppe Symphony Orchestra under Pierre Monteux, little thinking that in the following year it would be brought to an abrupt end by the outbreak of the Great War.

A rather curious thing happened to him in 1914: he was given a scholarship at the Royal College of Music. The offer was fully appreciated, of course, but he felt that to accept it would prejudice his professional career, for he was already becoming well-known as a soloist, so he asked the committee of the Patron's Fund if, instead of the scholarship, he could be given a grant to the value of it in order to pay off the balance that was still owing to a dealer for his Guadagnini violin. To his surprise, this most unusual suggestion was adopted.

Sammons's repertoire had by this time been enriched by a work that he particularly loved: the violin concerto by Sir Edward Elgar. This superb composition, of which he was later to become the world's greatest exponent, had been written in 1910 for Kreisler but had not, unfortunately, become very well known. At the outbreak of the Great War, Kreisler, who was later to join the Austrian army, was not available to play the concerto, and the musical world looked to Albert Sammons as being the only violinist who was capable of giving a satisfactory performance of it. Nothing could have pleased the English violinist more, and he gave up a great deal of his time to the study and practice of this superb work. It would be impossible to record the innumerable occasions upon which Sammons has won an ovation with it, but it is significant that Elgar himself said that no one seemed to get to the heart of the concerto as Sammons did. Writing to the soloist after a performance of it a few years ago, John Barbirolli, the eminent conductor, declared: "We felt privileged to be associated with you in the performance of the Elgar, which will live long in our memories".

It was during the Great War, when so many of the foreign violinists would not visit this country, that the British musical public began to realize that Albert Sammons had "arrived" as a virtuoso of the front rank, and had done so without calling himself Sammonstein. That world-famous violinist Ysaÿe exclaimed: "At last England has a great violinist," when he heard Sammons play at Lord Curzon's house. Other distinguished musicians present on this occasion were Lionel Tertis, who has done more to reveal the charm of the viola than any other string-player of the past or present, and Arthur Rubinstein, the Polish pianist.

Soon after his enlistment as a private in the Great War, Sammons found himself transferred to the Grenadier Guards, and while he was in this regiment he led the strings of its orchestra and played the clarinet in the military band. He had never pretended to play the clarinet, by the way, but a good musician can accomplish all sorts of strange musical tasks in an emergency, and with a few months' practice he was able to play all the marches and "selections" beloved by the band.

As soon as he returned to civilian life he resumed his concert work, and before we go any further, mention must be made of the important tours he made with William Murdoch giving sonata recitals. These were widely appreciated, and did much to enhance the prestige of both musicians.

Not long after the end of the Great War, Albert Sammons became very concerned at the inordinately large number of foreign musicians who were pouring into this country and taking concert engagements from the British musician. No one would wish to prevent a reasonable number of first-rate musicians from visiting England, and few begrudge them the fees they earn, although it may be said here that the astronomic fees demanded by some of them are not always in keeping with either their ability or their respect for the music they play. But in the early years of the "last peace", conditions were as bad for the professional musician as they are for the public in general to-day, and as more and more of these foreign artists arrived to snap up what few engagements there were, it became necessary for representatives of the English musicians to take action. Accordingly, Albert Sammons and a number of other artists, approached the Ministry of Labour and demanded some sort of official restraint upon these foreign visitors. Imagine the horror and disgust felt by the indignant deputation when a lofty civil servant informed them coldly that while the Ministry of Labour sympathized with them, very little could be done "because it would appear that there are no great English musicians." Albert Sammons has never forgotten that, and is therefore not very sympathetic towards those who believe that English music will never flourish until the art is nationalized and all musicians become civil servants.

The name of Albert Sammons has become so linked with the Elgar Concerto in the minds of music-lovers, that some are apt to overlook another famous concerto with which he will always be associated. This is that superb work by Delius, which, because of its difficulty, is liable to become neglected. When it was first completed the composer took it to Sammons for an expert opinion upon the solo part. The violinist made a careful study of it and then suggested a considerable number of amendments, particularly as some passages were quite unplayable. His suggestions were cordially welcomed by the composer, and a revised version was prepared, which, as many music-lovers are aware, is the one that was used when Sammons recorded the concerto for Columbia with the Liverpool Philharmonic Orchestra under Dr. Malcolm Sargent. Commenting upon his performance, Delius said: "You played wonderfully, and with such thorough understanding and poetic feeling." He once declared that Beecham, Eugene Goossens and Albert Sammons were among the few who understood him and could properly interpret his music.

Another concerto in which Sammons always shone —one uses the past tense because he has now given up concerto work—was the Brahms. After a performance of it with the BBC Symphony Orchestra Sir Adrian Boult wrote to him: "I can honestly say I never enjoyed a performance of the Brahms more." That, incidentally, was twenty years after he had first played it during the Great War, when the critics even then said that his performance ranked with the best from abroad.

Then of course there is the Beethoven Concerto, which has at all times held a place of honour in his

repertoire. He has played it over a hundred times—
and seventy of them were during the Second World
War! This concerto, and the Elgar, Delius and Brahms,
take first place among his "specialities", though he
deeply loves the Mozart, Bach and Mendelssohn
concertos, and has given some fine interpretations of
them.

About the ever-popular Mendelssohn Concerto he
has strong views: first it is, and always will be, one of
the finest compositions ever written for the violin,
despite the sneers of those who invariably regard as
worthless everything that appeals to the "ordinary
listener"; and secondly, it is a very difficult work to
play well, notwithstanding the number of people who
regard it as one of those works that can be ripped off
without a rehearsal. "There are more bad performances
of the Mendelssohn Concerto by world-famous artists
than of any other work in the repertoire of the instrument", Sammons declares.

In a recent discussion with the author, he said that
in his opinion the new Bartók concerto was very fine
music but not a successful *violin* concerto in the sense
that the Bloch concerto is, since Bartók apparently
overlooked the smallness of the violin tone in contrast
with that of the full orchestra. In this concerto the solo
fiddle can be heard properly only if the orchestra is
subdued to such an extent that much of the beauty
of the "architecture" is lost. A great pity, because
performances in which the conductor has to restrain
the orchestra the whole time with an iron hand are
seldom very successful. In broadcast performances
the soloist can, of course, be brought nearer the microphone, but that brings us to the thorny subject of
"balance and control" which seems to be a perpetual
perplexity with dozens of artists who broadcast regularly.

Like many of his fellow artists, Sammons feels some
concern about the degree of scope given to engineers
and others who are allowed to exercise control between

the microphone and transmitter, as it were. (Strictly speaking, the placing of the microphone is a far more important part of their work than the actual knob-twiddling.) Too often is the balance between the soloist and the accompanist far from perfect, indeed, there have been occasions when the result has been little short of ludicrous. Are these officials always qualified to exercise such tremendous and vital "control"? Do they not work too much by "rule of thumb" methods? There is a strong feeling among musicians that the BBC should attend to this matter much more conscientiously if it is to avoid charges of vandalism in the future. Some of its outside broadcasts have been really incredible, notably relays from the Albert Hall, certain provincial halls and cathedrals. We have heard orchestras and choirs that seemed to be almost devoid of certain important sections, soloists that seemed to be nearly half-a-mile away, and, worst of all, ensembles that seemed to consist almost entirely of percussion instruments! The old stock retort: "It must be your set" has long been refuted because dozens of people with excellent up-to-date receivers have complained on similar occasions.

In a discussion on this subject Albert Sammons said he felt that the average "balance" test in the studio was sometimes far too casual, and rarely took into account the vast difference between an accompaniment that consists of heavy clumps of chords and that which is made up of only a line or two of counterpoint. In the latter case the accompanist could be much nearer the soloist.

The same questions arise in the making of gramophone records, though conditions are improving, and the companies do seem more anxious to get first-class results nowadays. Sammons has vivid memories of a recording he made some years ago with William Murdoch. They had been asked to record a Schubert sonata for a certain company and had spent a great deal of time in private rehearsal to get it as near perfect as was humanly possible. In this particular work there was a very delicate passage that had to be played in a gentle, tranquil manner, but before they had played more than a dozen bars of it in the recording studio they were stopped by the engineer in charge who said that they would have to play it much louder, and with more "body", otherwise he would not pass it. The two soloists were most willing to oblige, but were steadfastly resolved not to do anything that would alter the character of the work, for their professional reputations were involved. After repeating the passage much in their original manner it was apparently approved by the engineer, but it was not until the records were on sale in the shops that they discovered that the engineer had taken matters into his own hands entirely, and had amplified the section concerned to such an extent that it sounded almost like a cornet solo! Then, on top of this, one of the critics, in his review of the record, told Sammons that if he couldn't play Schubert properly he ought to leave it alone!

On another occasion Albert Sammons encountered an engineer of that good-natured but very patronizing type who regards all musicians as temperamental, mentally deficient children who have to be patted on the head and fobbed off with bland assurances that everything will be all right. A recording he had made was played back to him, and he felt genuinely alarmed at the undue volume of his solo part, which again should have been very delicate and serene. "Is that really what the volume will be like on the finished records?" he asked incredulously. "Oh no!" the engineer laughed, "don't you worry, Mr. Sammons, we shall get it three or four times louder than that before we've finished with it!"

Conditions are not so bad to-day, of course, but Sammons still wonders whether it is fair to judge any musician from his recordings and broadcasts, for apart from the general expression, so many little subtleties in the playing of a fine artist who has spent months, even years, in the study of a particular work, can be "smoothed out" by a man who is more interested in electricity or mechanics than music.

Noteworthy among the recordings made by Albert Sammons are those of the Delius Violin Concerto made with the Liverpool Philharmonic Orchestra under Sir Malcolm Sargent (Columbia) and of the Mozart *Concertante Sinfonie* for violin and viola (K.364) made with Lionel Tertis and the London Philharmonic Orchestra conducted by the late Sir Hamilton Harty (Columbia). For the same company he has also recorded Dvořák's *Humoreske*.

In his time, Sammons has played under almost every conductor of importance in the world. One can well imagine the rich experience gained from contact with such a wide variety of musicians: Sir Thomas Beecham, Sir Edward Elgar, Sir Henry J. Wood, Sir Adrian Boult, Sir Hamilton Harty, Sir Landon Ronald, John Barbirolli, Sir Malcolm Sargent, Mengelberg, Nikish, Safonov, Ernaldi, Monteux, Bruno Walter, and so forth. What a range of musical style is brought to mind as one reads those names! Sammons has happy memories of all of them, as he has of the many composers he has been privileged to know, and as far as one can gather, his only complaint is that some of the British conductors tend to show far more respect to artists with foreign names than they do towards English soloists.

Just as he is a ready champion for the cause of the British performer, Sammons is proud of the great composers that have done so much to raise our reputation in the world of music: Elgar, Delius, Vaughan Williams, Bax, Moeran, Bliss, John Ireland, Walton, Benjamin Britten; all these, he declares, and many more, compare favourably with any foreign composers of their generation. It is significant that the last four concertos he played were those of Delius, Dyson, Elgar and Moeran.

He also attaches great importance to the teaching of the rising generation of musicians, and many a good violinist of the future will be grateful for the fact that Albert Sammons has regarded it as a duty to set aside a definite proportion of his time to the training of the artists who will succeed him. He is a Fellow of the Royal College of Music, and is keenly interested in his professorial work. Thomas Matthews and Winifred Roberts were his pupils, and a very promising young artist in his care to-day is Alan Loveday.

Sammons is himself of no particular "school" in music, and believes that it is up to every artist to develop his own personality. He has several ideas that have been described as "revolutionary" and has evolved a system of training using exercises that have the effect of concentrating all the best methods of the older masters. Most violinists are acquainted with his *Virtuosic Studies* and *The Secret of Fine Technique*.

His advice to young players is "Concentrate upon perfect intonation. You will never distinguish yourself until your intonation is perfect, for it is this and artistic interpretation that marks the difference between the work of the great violinist and the mediocre. Bad intonation is the student's greatest fault."

He is very modest about his accomplishments as a composer, yet his Phantasy String Quartet in B won him the Cobbett Chamber Music Prize some years ago. He has written a number of pleasant little violin solos that reveal a decided talent for writing effectively for his instrument.

Sammons uses a superb Matteo Gofriller fiddle dated 1696. This beautiful instrument by the Venetian contemporary of Stradivarius has been his constant companion for the past twenty years. Previous to that he used a Strad, but he prefers his present instrument. He has several other fiddles which need not be mentioned here, and is quite a connoisseur of all types of stringed instruments.

Now a final word about him in general. Fame and honours have left "our own Albert" quite unaffected, and he has little use for the snobs of the musical world. No airs or graces, no "arty" poses, no affectations, no precious or "clever" theories spoil him: he can chat for half-an-hour to any member of the orchestra without making the latter feel self-conscious. And if you happen to overhear him talking to Jim or Bill or Charlie you will more likely hear him saying something about sport than attempting to describe that marvellous but unpublished quarter-tone rhapsody written by that unknown but frightfully clever young man who wears yellow trousers. It is twelve years since he played golf, but there are plenty of his friends who remember what a formidable rival he could be on the course. And in the "nineteenth hole" they still tell you the classic story of the newspaper reporter who interviewed Sammons one year when he won the championship at Bognor and gave a recital there the same evening. "But doesn't your golf interfere with your fiddle-playing, Mr. Sammons?" the journalist asked. "No," came the reply, "on the contrary, my fiddle-playing is apt to interfere with my golf."

COLIN SAUER

AMONG the rising generation of solo violinists Colin Sauer is unique. He is not only an able musician but a personality with a most unusual intellect, and it is going to be interesting to watch his career. In the struggle towards the front rank, the young artist of to-day has little time for anything but practice, practice and yet more practice. He may snatch an evening off to hear an internationally-famed virtuoso, but that evening will be spent in shrewd observation and critical listening solely with the object of gleaning knowledge that will be useful. He may read the life of a great composer, but he will probably be making notes for future use before he has got through the first few chapters. He may spend an evening at a cinema and allow his brain to be drugged for a few hours with synthetic sentiment, but he will walk home bitterly regretting the fact that he could have rehearsed half-a-dozen sonatas in the time he has wasted. Or he may even take a young lady for a walk across Hampstead Heath, but the conversation will almost certainly be of music or of other things they hope to do when music provides them with sufficient income to get married.

It is unfortunately true that many musicians possess, or develop, one-track minds. But the explanation is quite a simple one: unless he is a jazz-merchant, the musician of to-day has to train himself up to a high standard of proficiency—and keep himself there. To do that he is not likely to have much time for anything else before he reaches the age of thirty. After that age, he probably doesn't bother about thinking of anything else. There is, however, one other factor that must be borne in mind: unlike certain other professions—law, medicine, literature, for instance—music does not encourage its servants to mix with the "laity" or to understand them. A man could become a superb violinist or singer without even attempting to probe into the problems of humanity, but he would be a singularly unsuccessful doctor or lawyer. It is true that music takes the artist far afield, but how much does the travelling virtuoso learn of the cities and people he visits? Many an artist has assured us that there is little difference between an audience in Manchester and one in Munich, and at least one has had the impression of playing before nothing but rows and rows of codfish. Music, therefore, is conducive to a form of narrow-mindedness that is of no service to art in general. It is an occupational disease to which certain sections of the profession are more susceptible than others. Composers, it seems, are comparatively free of the infection—but are not immune.

Colin Sauer is one of the few young solo artists who plan their lives so that their intellects develop with their artistic accomplishments. But that does not make him unique, because others who may be numbered among "the few" also appear in this volume. Where he stands quite alone, however, is that he studies, among other things, dogmatic theology!

Despite his foreign-sounding name, he is a typical example of a cultured young Englishman, and his parents are entirely British. He was born at Ilford on 13 July 1924, and knew nothing of the violin until he started learning to play it in a school class at the age of nine. A year later he won a scholarship awarded by the National Union of School Orchestras which enabled him to make a further study of the violin in a class held by that organisation at the Guildhall School of Music. His progress was so remarkable that he was soon afterwards chosen to play solos at the concerts held by the National Union of School Orchestras at the Albert Hall.

Meanwhile, he was receiving a general education at the County High School, Ilford. Mathematics was his best subject, but some idea of his general intelligence may be gathered from the fact that he gained nine credits in the London Matriculation, and this was in spite of all those little setbacks caused by the war, evacuation and whatnot. In passing, it might be added that he gave frequent recitals at school and, of course, took part in all the other music-making activities there.

During his evacuation he was able to continue his study of music, and in due course he won a scholarship to the Royal Academy of Music, which decided for him the matter of a career. He studied there under Rowsby Woof and Frederick Grinke, and responded so well to their instruction that soon after his admission to the Academy he was able to accept orchestral engagements. One of the first was with the New London Orchestra under Alec Sherman, but he was soon to accept an appointment with the Boyd Neel Orchestra that was to last over two years. Useful experience was also gained when he was given opportunities of deputizing in the London Philharmonic and Hallé Orchestras.

Orchestral experience alone, however, is not sufficient for a violinist aspiring to solo rank, and Sauer wisely accepted an appointment as second fiddle in the Aeolian Quartet. For two years he played with this ensemble giving many recitals and quite a number of broadcasts, but, in turn, this appointment had to be relinquished when he decided to specialize in solo work, since it would have been impossible to work up an adequate repertoire in the small amount of spare time he then had available.

At first he was content to gain experience as a soloist in the provinces and with amateur orchestras, but in a surprisingly short time he was appearing with good professional string orchestras, such as Kathleen Riddick's excellent ensemble, and at all manner of chamber concerts, including that remarkable series at the National Gallery. And here the reader must be introduced to his sister Sheila, a talented pianist three years his junior, who has proved herself to be an able accompanist whenever she has appeared with her brother. Another young musician of interest who has frequently accompanied Colin Sauer is Ronald Smith, a promising composer. Sauer gave the first performance of his violin concerto at the Academy under the direction of Clarence Raybould a few years ago.

The first important recital given by Sauer in London was at the Wigmore Hall on 17 October 1946; an event that drew considerable attention to him even though he was then at that awkward age when he could be considered neither as a youthful prodigy nor a mature artist. Still, as the editor of *The Strad* put it, he showed his large audience that he was in quite a different category from the usual "promising young fiddler". The appropriateness of this remark was proved at another recital he gave at the same hall during the following summer, when his programme included works by Handel, Bach, Grieg, Achron, Bartók, Delius and Nováček.

Sauer's concerto repertoire is now being rapidly expanded, but it already includes the three Bach concertos, the Mendelssohn, Beethoven, Brahms, Lalo, Tchaikovsky, Bruch, Sibelius and Vaughan Williams (*accademico*), and by the time this book appears in print the list will probably be quite a lengthy one.

The qualities that mark his playing are reliable intonation and the absence of the roughness that so often mars the work of young players. He uses aluminium-covered A and D strings and the customary silver-covered G. Of the violinists of to-day he regards Heifetz as the paragon, but considers that Szigeti has few equals in the playing of Bach, and that for sheer technique Ida Haendel stands alone, in this country at any rate.

One reason why Sauer's intonation is so good is that he has an unusually acute faculty for hearing music mentally before he attempts to play it: a quality possessed by all good conductors; in fact, one that is indispensable to anybody who aspires to conduct. He finds that he makes the best progress by playing very short sessions of practice and doing a great deal of thinking in between. Nevertheless, he is always trying to discover the ideal method of practice: he finds it almost impossible to concentrate properly for any great length of time, and that practice without such concentration is of little value. By the ordinary vague and haphazard type of practice, anything up to nine-tenths of one's time can be entirely wasted.

Sauer finds that the best way to make steady progress is to concentrate upon one detail or action of playing at a time—intonation, bowing, and so forth. He has discovered that as soon as he is sure of the intonation, a great deal can be done by practising the left hand alone. Some of his friends are amused at the methodical way in which he plans his rehearsing: he allocates a certain amount of time to each particular item and stops immediately he reaches the end of each period regardless of whether or not the piece has been sufficiently polished. He finds that on the following day he can quite easily pick up the threads again where he left off.

Typical of this young artist is his belief that life itself is even more wonderful than music. He deplores the narrow-mindedness, the limited vision, of the average executive musician, and insists that a musician cannot develop as a true artist unless he tries to understand the world outside his own little sphere; unless he is willing to grapple with the problems of life.

Sauer takes a great interest in education and is convinced that, despite the grandiose schemes of the planners of to-day (they look so impressive on paper but are so miserable in practice), we have an enormous amount still to learn about the imparting of knowledge to the young.

His reading of theology is no mere affectation: having passed through the atheistic and agnostic stages he is now a keen reader of Christian apologetics and will travel miles to hear any preacher who has something important to say, regardless of his denomination. Incidentally, Sauer is always having terrific arguments with his fellow musicians about religion. Evolution is also a subject that used to occupy his thoughts a great deal but lately it has been supplanted by philosophy, psychology and logic! (One hopes he will stay on these broad and stable lines, and not start toying with the "isms", which have proved to be the undoing of more than one good musician.)

Having sketched the best part of a reference library into this profile of Colin Sauer, it is now necessary only to add the athletic touch—only in this case it is more of a splash than a touch, for while he was a schoolboy he was as crazy about cricket as any youngster in the first eleven, in fact for many years he wanted to become a County cricketer! He was destined, however, not for Lords but for Wimbledon, since the bat gave way to the racquet during the early years of adolescence. At fifteen he was accepted for the Junior Wimbledon, and he might have become a white-flannelled hero in at least one of the glossy weeklies had not a slight accident in the summer of 1946 checked his enthusiasm for the game: he strained a ligament in his right hand and was warned that a repetition of it would seriously affect his violin-playing.

And now, as he has occupied more of our space than some of the violinists of international repute, we must bid him a hasty, if regretful, farewell.

(Left)

TOSCHA
SEIDEL
(as a young man)

Gramophone Co.

(Right)

JACQUES
THIBAUD

Studio Carlet Aine

Robin A

MARIE WILSON

have our individuality once play within its limits. Allowing for limits, if once I came to a passage I demanded an especially beautiful tone to render it, he would say: 'Never mind the beauty here. The cantabile begins the moment you are rid of perfect bowing, and as he often said, 'There must be no such things as strings and bow in the tonality; consequently one must not play the violin, one must sing the violin.'"

TOSCHA SEIDEL

AS a contrast to the precise and restrained style of several of our leading violinists of to-day, Toscha Seidel's playing is remarkable in its emotion: the artist in him dominates everything, and he plays with a passion rarely found in modern musicians. His rich, warm tone can be sweet and gentle in a slow movement, bold and virile in the next, and can culminate in a fiery climax, yet all the time it seems to keep its own peculiarly spiritual character.

Like Milstein, he came originally from the Russian city of Odessa, where he was born on 4 November 1900. His father was a local business man; his mother a schoolteacher, and but for the existence of an uncle who was an accomplished professional violinist, we might look in vain into his family history for musical antecedents of any distinction. But like so many Russians of the middle-class in those easy-going days, his parents were genuinely interested in music, and gave their son every encouragement when he displayed promise as a violinist. His first teacher was Max Fiedelmann, but in due course he was sent to study at the Stern Conservatorium in Berlin.

Seidel was also a pupil of the renowned Auer, and in Saleski's *Famous Musicians of a Wandering Race* there is quoted a statement made by him concerning his master's methods. It runs:

"Professor Auer always taught us to play as individuals, and while he never allowed us to overstep the boundaries of the musically aesthetic, he

M   163

gave our individuality free play within its limits. When playing for him, if once I came to a passage which demanded an especially beautiful legato rendering, he would say: 'Now show how you can sing!' The exquisite legato he taught was all a matter of perfect bowing, and as he often said, 'There must be no such things as strings and hair in the pupil's consciousness: one must not play the violin; one must sing the violin'."

Seidel made his début in 1915 when he played the Tchaikovsky Concerto at Christiania, as Oslo was then called. This led to a series of concerts in Scandinavia and Leningrad that launched him on a successful career. In his early youth he was so much in demand that his mother became anxious for his general education, which was in danger of being somewhat neglected, so during those first few tours, and even on his initial visit to America, she engaged a German professor to go with him and coach him in general educational subjects.

For a year or two, Seidel's popularity was confined to Norway, Sweden and certain Russian cities, but his American début was a great triumph and brought him almost at once into the ranks of international celebrities. The late H. E. Krehbiel, writing in the New York *Tribune*, declared:

"In dash and fire, breadth of bowing, solidity and richness of tone, his performance was unforgettable."

A similar success was his first appearance in London. The critic of the *Daily Mail* remarked that:

"Kreisler at his best did not play the Brahms Concerto with more animated passion than this youth, who showed no intimidation at its oppressive traditions, rather handling it heartily, whereby the music lived more warmly."

Then he embarked upon world tours that took him almost all over the globe: he has been heard in every

European musical centre of any importance (in Paris, especially, he has won many an ovation), and he has found favour in Australia and New Zealand as well as the Far East.

America, however, was the country in which he found the greatest scope, and it is not surprising that he decided to settle there and to take American citizenship. He was naturalized in 1924, and now has a beautiful home in California where he frequently entertains his many musical friends. His marriage to Estelle Manheim took place on 1 January 1929.

Seidel has always been a popular broadcaster, and for several years was the musical advisory director to the Columbia Broadcasting System. His taste in music is conservative, but he is not at all narrow-minded or biased, and can be relied upon to pass a shrewd opinion upon any type of music. Beethoven and Mozart are probably his favourite composers, but it is significant that he regards the Brahms Violin Concerto to be the finest work ever written for his instrument.

In person he bears little resemblance to the average man's idea of a professional musician: he is a short but well-built figure fond of outdoor activities, especially golf, swimming, yachting and driving one of those enormously powerful cars that look like a cross between a speedboat and an aeroplane. As a diversion from music he reads a great deal of scientific literature and dabbles in photography.

Films also appeal strongly to him, and just before the Second World War he was associated for some time with Metro-Goldwyn-Mayer. It will probably be recalled that he recorded the sound-track of the Intermezzo in the film *Escape to Happiness*, which featured Leslie Howard and Ingrid Bergman. To satisfy public demand, he afterwards made an ordinary gramophone record of this little Intermezzo, which is called *Souvenir de Vienne*.

One more point of biographical interest: in the summer of 1942 Seidel joined the U.S. Navy, and finding himself in the company of a few members of the Los Angeles Philharmonic Orchestra, he organized a string quartet. Facilities for practising were given to them at their training station, and for some time afterwards they gave regular recitals to sailors in the naval hospital. As a result of this activity he was later appointed assistant bandmaster and soloist at the naval training station at San Diego, California.

JOSEPH SZIGETI

THE name of Szigeti has already been mentioned several times in this book, chiefly by those of his contemporaries who greatly admire his "steel and velvet" tone, as one critic has described it. His approach to his art is essentially an intellectual one, and consequently he enjoys the esteem not only of the greater critics but of most modern composers, whose works he interprets with understanding and scrupulous care. His non-emotional manner of playing is apt to leave some listeners unmoved, and one occasionally hears it said that his "cerebral" interpretations lack feeling, but no one can deny that he is a great artist, and few would really wish him to modify the style that he has made his own.

He was born at Budapest on 5 September 1892, taught by his father with the assistance of an uncle, and in due course was admitted to the Budapest Royal Academy of Music, where he became a pupil of that fine Hungarian violinist Jenö Hubay (1858-1937). Hubay's class was a bewildering collection of prodigies bent upon mastering the technicalities of violin-playing in the shortest possible time so that they could satisfy the ambitions of their parents, but it was the best training ground available to Szigeti at the time, and he was only twelve years old when he had the honour of playing to Joachim, who was deeply impressed by his skill and gave him every encouragement.

A year later he appeared at a public concert held at the Budapest Academy, and shortly afterwards made a successful début in Berlin. Then in 1906 he came to England, and made his home here for over six years.

His London début at the Bechstein (now Wigmore) Hall was approved by many of our more discriminating musicians, but caused little stir in the press, probably on account of the number of boy prodigies that were then being thrust before the public. The *Musical Times* dismissed the recital in three lines thus: "Joska Szigeti, another Hungarian violinist prodigy, made his first appearance in England at the Bechstein Hall on 24 May with the usual success." However, he then embarked upon a tour of the provinces and from time to time made many more highly-successful appearances in London, often in the distinguished company of such people as Busoni, Backhaus and Melba.

In passing it should be said that he was a perfectly normal boy who lived a happy, healthy life. There was nothing of the pampered darling about him, and he was not made to live in the "hot-house" atmosphere enjoyed by the average child prodigy.

As he grew up he transformed himself from the usual gifted child into an adult artist with a great deal more success than is usually the case: his musical intuition developed amazingly, and people began to realize that here was "a virtuoso with a difference."

In 1917 he succeeded Henri Marteau (1874-1934), the distinguished French violinist and composer, as professor of the violin at the Geneva Conservatoire, and stayed there seven years, during which time he was frequently engaged as soloist for the Nikisch concerts in Berlin and important musical events in almost all the other capitals of Europe, including Paris, Brussels, Budapest, Bucharest, Stockholm, Madrid, Amsterdam, etc. At these he played under most of the greatest conductors of the day.

He was still in Geneva when Leopold Stokowski, conductor of the famous Philadelphia Orchestra, became interested in him, having heard highly complimentary reports of his playing, and invited him to make a concert tour of the United States. Szigeti accepted, and made his American début with that eminent conductor and his orchestra at Philadelphia in the autumn of 1925. Then he went on to win fresh laurels in New York, where he was well received, but owing to his peculiar style of playing, without evoking the somewhat hysterical enthusiasm that was then being lavished upon one or two of the more popular violinists. His reserved and scholarly manner did not appeal to the popular journalists, for instance, so he did not get any of those splashy "write-ups" that tend to stampede the public in the direction of the box-office. The better critics, on the other hand, wrote most appreciatively of his performance, drawing attention to the different phases of his artistry that were revealed as he changed from one type of music to another. (His programme had consisted of works by Tartini, Bach, Mozart, Bloch, Prokofiev, Veracini, Dvořák, Kreisler and Paganini.)

So Szigeti built up his reputation as a scholarly violinist, and was content to rise slowly upon the good-will of the discriminating musician. By 1930 he was world-famous, having given recitals in almost every country of importance and been decorated by the French Government, who appointed him to the Legion of Honour, a rare award to a foreign musician.

During the next few years he went twice round the world giving concerts at hundreds of musical centres. Frequent visits were made to the Far East and over a dozen to the Soviet Union. In England it was probably his playing of Sir Hamilton Harty's Concerto (which was dedicated to him) that first established him, and he was soon to play under all our great conductors. Sir Henry J. Wood and Sir Thomas Beecham both recognized his unusual merits.

Many a music-lover will remember the recitals

Szigeti gave with Melba and John McCormack, but now his frequent visits here and excellent broadcasts have won him a greater public than ever before.

During the Second World War he maintained his musical activities, but had one or two narrow escapes, as, for instance, when he gave up his reservation on an air-liner to an officer in the American Army. The 'plane crashed and all its passengers were killed.

Szigeti is one of the most interesting personalities in music to-day: he is full of ideas and his interpretations are always interesting: many a time has he revealed some new beauty in a work that has always been over-looked by the majority of violinists, while his perform-ances are invariably stimulating. His readings are sometimes quite unusual, and have even caused surprise in the past, but there is always a well-reasoned explanation whenever he diverges from tradition.

Nothing pleases Szigeti more than to give a recital in which he can introduce his audience to something new, or revive some work that has been unwarrantably neglected. To give a list of all such works would be impossible here, but it is worth mentioning that many contemporary composers have shown their esteem by dedicating new works to him, notably Bartók (Rhapsody for violin and orchestra, and the Rhapsody for violin, clarinet and piano), Bloch (*Nuit exotique*), Ysaÿe (violin sonata), and Prokofiev (Sonata in D major). The last-named was first performed in England by Szigeti on 25 August 1946.

Programme-building is an art in which Szigeti has few rivals: he spends a great deal of time in choosing his pieces, and arranges them in his programmes not merely in chronological order, as many artists do, but with special consideration for their mood and density. He believes that the order in which half-a-dozen pieces are played can be just as important as the manner in which an artist would display the same number of

COLIN
SAUER

Bernard Bennett

EFREM ZIMBALIST

JOSEPH
SZIGETI

RAYMOND COHEN

paintings upon a wall. Young violinists, especially, are apt to overlook the fact that a piece of music can be "killed" by an ill-chosen work immediately following it, just as the effect of a picture can be utterly spoilt by having an incongruous painting at its side. The dominant work of a programme should be preceded by pieces that lead up to it in a suitable manner. Now that audiences are becoming more discriminating and sensitive these seemingly unimportant details should never be overlooked.

His repertoire is enormous, and includes an imposing list of modern works as well as many of the best classics. When Bloch wrote his violin concerto he was insistent that Szigeti should give the first performance of it, because he felt that in the hands of this fine artist it would certainly receive sympathetic treatment. Szigeti gave the first European performance of this work on 9 March 1947 at a Philharmonic Concert under Sir Thomas Beecham.

Prokofiev has always regarded Szigeti as his finest interpreter, and Bartók used to speak very highly of his readings. It would, however, be wrong to imagine that Szigeti's style is suited only to modern works, for it is readily adaptable to any style of composition. Although he is so successful with modern music he does not believe in specialization, which, he feels, is bound to limit one's artistic faculties, and when one hears him playing, say, the Brahms Concerto (of which he has given well over 150 performances) one realizes that he does not attempt to stamp it with his own style. He plays this concerto with an understanding that reveals a deep insight into the spirit of the work. He is not interested in self-glorification.

Similarly, although no violinist could have more up-to-date ideas about his art, he freely acknowledges that he has never forgotten the inspiration he received as a boy from the playing of Joachim. He has the greatest respect for tradition, but does not make a fetish of it.

He is said to possess "the most elegant right arm of living violinists", and listeners will probably have observed that he keeps it closer to his body than most violinists do to-day. Some teachers would severely criticize this, but it does not prevent him from achieving a wonderful elasticity. His left hand is amazingly accurate. The steely strength and smoothness of his style is particularly enjoyable in Bach: one cannot help feeling that the great organist would have beamed with joy if he could have heard Szigeti's delightfully clean playing of his works.

The recordings he has made for Columbia include the Beethoven Concerto with the British Symphony Orchestra conducted by Bruno Walter; the Brahms Concerto with the Hallé Orchestra under Sir Hamilton Harty; and with the London Philharmonic Orchestra conducted by Sir Thomas Beecham, the Mendelssohn, Prokofiev and Mozart No. 4 concertos. With Carl Flesch he also recorded the Bach D minor Concerto for two violins accompanied by an orchestra under Walter Goehr.

Szigeti is tall and slim, and is never troubled by "nerves". He advises young violinists to do no more than two hours' practice a day—but that must be really intensive and intelligent practice. This period of work should be preceded by mental preparation of the music to be played, for it is useless to start the "mechanics" of playing until one has a complete mental impression of the work. Diligent study of the music before the fiddle is taken in hand is one of the secrets of great artistry. One's style must of course be adapted to the type of work one is attempting: nobody plays Bach as they would Tchaikovsky, but people are less clear about the differences between other types of composer.

He would remind ambitious young violinists that the life of the virtuoso is not an easy one, and because one often has to rehearse in an icy-cold hall immediately upon arrival and without the sustenance of even a light meal beforehand, he recommends that students should make a habit of rising at six o'clock, even on winter mornings, and practising for an hour before break-fast!

As one would imagine, he is a man of intellect, and can converse upon many subjects other than music. He is interested in science, art and literature, and reads a great deal, believing that a good background of general culture is indispensable to any musician. Too many musicians reveal in their playing that they are men of sadly limited interests, men with one-track minds whose knowledge of life is pitifully small. He is rarely bored: even the enormous amount of travelling he is compelled to do is a source of interest and enlightenment to him. The true artist, he believes, must know something of the world beyond his own little sphere.

Szigeti is a great conversationalist, and can be extremely witty. He loves good company, and is never supercilious. Good dance music is always pleasant to him, and he has no snobbish feelings towards those who play it. When he wanted a really competent clarinettist to share with him the honour of giving the first perform-ance of Bartók's Rhapsody for clarinet, violin and piano he had no hesitation in choosing Benny Goodman, despite this able musician's reputation as a dance-band leader.

He is fond of cricket and takes an interest in a variety of sports, believing that they have a cultural value.

His recently-completed autobiography, *With Strings Attached*, has been published in New York by Knopf, but up to the time of writing has not yet appeared in this country. We are told that he wrote it "the hard way", that is, with neither secretary nor typewriter, chiefly in railway coaches. It is an absorbing collection of reminiscences that provide sidelights upon such diverse personalities as Stravinsky, Bartók, Duke Ellington, Thomas Mann, Benny Goodman, Albert Einstein, etc., and is rich in anecdote. He recalls the "indolent, languorous grace" of Melba's singing, the Wanamaker concerts by selected players using instruments from the famed collection, the amusing sight of Goldmark patiently soaking the stamps off return envelopes sent hopefully by autograph hunters doomed to disappointment, and those words written to him by Busoni: "May your art satisfy you: others will rejoice in it, but the former is the more important."

JACQUES THIBAUD

THIS eminent virtuoso is generally regarded as the great master of the French school of violin playing, and has appropriately been described as "a Parisian to his fingertips".

He was born at Bordeaux on 27 September 1880, son of a local violinist and teacher of music. Being unduly sensitive to music he was by far the keenest of his father's pupils. His father was very anxious that he should distinguish himself as a pianist and accordingly kept the lad at the keyboard until he was seven years old. Then, however, his course in music was changed, for he was taken to a symphony concert and heard the Beethoven Violin Concerto for the first time. It was an experience so moving that before the end of the work he was in tears: never before had a musical instrument spoken to him with such feeling. He went home carrying a vivid impression of the soloist in his mind, and resolved that somehow he, too, would play the violin in that manner.

Seeing that his son had fallen in love with the violin, the wise music teacher raised no objection to his new ambition; indeed, he gave him every encouragement, and within two years he had become quite an accomplished little violinist. At about this time, when he was nine years old, Eugène Ysaÿe heard him play and spoke very highly of his talent.

Nothing very startling was to happen during the next four years, however, and at the age of thirteen or fourteen he entered the Paris Conservatoire to become

a pupil of Marsick (1848-1924, a pupil of Joachim).
After two years with this Belgian violinist he won the
first prize for his instrument.

Although he was by then an excellent violinist, no
great opportunity came his way, and for two or three
years he was obliged to earn his living by accepting
quite humble engagements: in a café in the Latin
Quarter of Paris, for instance, and at the Concert
Rouge. It might be added that he never regretted
this experience as a rank-and-file musician.

When he was about seventeen he was offered a
place in the famous Colonne Orchestra, and came to the
notice of Edouard Colonne himself, who kindly offered
to give him further lessons. Under the guidance of
this able musician he made further progress, and the
opportunity for which he had waited came at last on a
Sunday when the leader of the orchestra happened to
be taken ill. Thibaud was delighted when he was asked
to fill the man's place, and as luck would have it, the
programme included the Saint-Saëns Prelude to *The
Deluge*, which contains a fine violin solo. In this Thibaud
made such a good impression that immediately after the
concert he received an engagement as a soloist. Within
a little while he was so heavily booked-up for solo work
that he was obliged to resign his orchestral appointment.

His début as a soloist was at the annual festival at
Anger, in 1898, and during the following season he
made well over fifty appearances supported by the
Colonne Orchestra. After this he simply leapt to fame,
as one may gather from the statement made by Ysaÿe,
who watched his career with the greatest interest:
"There are two violinists from whose playing I can
always be certain of learning something. They are
Kreisler and Thibaud."

Tours of France, England, Belgium, Germany,
Italy, Holland and other European countries, put
his name on the lips of many millions of music lovers,
and in 1903 he made his first visit to the United States.

His American début was made in New York with the Wetzler Orchestra, and he won high praise in the concertos of Mozart and Saint-Saëns.

Like most Frenchmen, Thibaud is a strong patriot at heart despite the cosmopolitan feeling that the travelling virtuoso is bound to acquire in time, and he was proud to serve his country during the Great War. With the French Army he spent nearly two years in the front lines, and was in action at Ypres, Champagne, Marne, Aisne, Arras and Verdun. After being wounded —fortunately not too seriously—he was taken to hospital and afterwards discharged.

Resuming his life as a touring virtuoso he soon found himself going further and further afield, and some idea of his travels may be gained from the fact that between the two world wars he visited such countries as China and Japan, India, South America and a dozen others. It should be noted, however, that during the Nazi régime he repeatedly refused to play in Germany. Many of his finest recitals have been given with his two brothers: Francis, a 'cellist of great merit, and Joseph, a masterly pianist.

During the Second World War he spent much of his time in writing his memoirs, and he also became a member of the French Intelligence Service because his knowledge of high-ranking persons in almost every country of the world proved to be of the utmost value.

Thibaud possesses an exquisite Pique which formerly belonged to Ysaÿe, and also plays upon a Vuillaume: a reproduction of "Le Messie". His finest instrument, however, is the superb 1709 Strad that was formerly used by another distinguished French violinist, Pierre Baillot (1771-1842).

His playing is remarkable for several outstanding qualities. The tone, for instance, is warm and mellow, yet of the utmost purity: he never indulges in that type of emotional playing that borders upon vulgarity. His bowing is supremely graceful. As one would imagine, he excels in the interpretation of French music—he has always made a speciality of it—but his playing of Bach, Mozart and Beethoven leaves little to be desired. Speaking generally, he seems more at home in highly-coloured works—the Saint-Saëns B minor Concerto, for instance—and those who heard him in London in the spring of 1945 will agree that his style is eminently suited to such works as Chausson's *Poème* and Lalo's *Symphonie Espagnole*. A point of interest is that Thibaud always likes to concentrate in silence upon the music he is to play for at least fifteen minutes before a concert. He is a very temperamental musician and even a slight disturbance can distract his attention, but "nerves" do not worry him.

He attaches great importance to the social value of music, and he believes that music has a special mission to take people's minds off the perplexities and sorrows of everyday life. For that reason he finds it difficult to be patient with those who insist that the chief purpose of modern music is to depict the ugliness and harshness of life to-day. People don't want to have their miseries and worries reflected in music: they want to get away from them.

Like Elman, Thibaud feels that one should not approach music in the critical frame of mind: it is a great mistake to go to a concert with the intention of finding fault and displaying one's "sensitivity" to imperfections as some people like to do. He has often sat in the audience when some well-meaning but not-too-well-accomplished musician has done his best to interpret a difficult work and been greatly irritated by the comments of "superior" people who find a fiendish joy in pouncing upon the slightest fault. They make no real effort to appreciate the music at all. Incidentally, artists of the standing of Thibaud, Heifetz, and so forth, are not flattered by the attendance of those who go to their concerts merely because their technique is supposed to be flawless. Thibaud believes that the true music-lover is one who goes to a concert in a mood conducive to the understanding of the music he is about to hear. An experienced musician can sense that mood quite easily and is more likely to give of his best than if he feels he is being regarded merely as a sort of wizard who has come to dazzle his audience with musical gymnastics.

Thibaud's great interest in chamber music is well known, and some of his finest recordings are those in which he joins with other distinguished artists in the performance of classical trios. There is, for instance, the Beethoven Trio in B-flat, Opus 97 (*The Arch-Duke*) in which he can be heard with Cortot and Casals, and with the same artists he has recorded the Haydn Trio in G major and the Schubert Trio No. 1 in B-flat, Opus 99. These three are H.M.V. recordings.

IN a north-country coal-pit during the "eighties" there worked a lad of seventeen or eighteen whose one great desire in life was to become a professional musician. He had decided talent—of that there was no doubt—but conditions in the coal mining areas in those days offered little encouragement to those who wished to practise an art as a livelihood. Life was grim; but so was the determination of this ambitious youth. Hours were long—very long indeed if judged by modern standards—and the work was utterly exhausting; yet this young man would go home and practise his fiddle hour after hour, often working into the early hours of the morning. Eventually, his perseverance was rewarded, and in due course he was able to come to London as a rank-and-file musician.

Having started somewhat later than usual, Wilson —for that was his name—saw that the chances of his fulfilling his ambition to become a solo artist were remote indeed, and as the years slipped by he became content to lead a life that had become agreeable to him: playing in the orchestras of London theatres. For many years he was the leader of the Gaiety Theatre orchestra.

In 1903 his wife bore him a daughter, Marie, and during the next few years he became more and more gratified to observe that his child had inherited his love of music. In time, too, it became evident that she was unusually gifted, for she began playing the violin with remarkable facility.

Believing that his daughter could succeed where he had failed; that she could reach the goal that was now too distant an objective for himself, he devoted several hours every day to her instruction. But a difficulty arose almost immediately. Like many a gifted child, Marie was restless and did not take kindly to the drudgery of practising on her fiddle for three or four hours a day. There were times when she loved the streams of melody that could be drawn from her instrument, but others when the wearisome playing of scales for hour after hour made her positively loathe the violin and everything connected with it. She had a will of her own, but so had her father, and being a man who had become accustomed to hard work, he was not going to let his daughter fritter away her time, so Marie had to do her daily practice whether she liked it or not.

It must have been when she was about six years old that she was given her first opportunity to play in public. She was not at all excited at the prospect, and her parents began to wonder what sort of inducement they could offer to make her work diligently for the event. At last her mother hit upon an idea that was to prove extremely useful during the ensuing years. Marie's interest in music had always taken second place to her love of good food, so her mother pointed out that at the concert there would be refreshments during the interval.

"Refreshments?" the child echoed, her mind conjuring up visions of iced cakes. There was now a new light of understanding in her eyes, "Oh, well then, perhaps it will be worth while. . . ."

It so happened that Marie had to play the item immediately before the interval. This she did, with exceptional skill, but scarcely had the sound of the last note left her instrument than with but a perfunctory nod to the audience for their generous applause she dashed from the stage with the words: "Now, Mum, where are those refreshments? . . ."

For years afterwards, her parents found that the easiest way to make Marie work for a concert was to assure her that the catering arrangements were in good hands.

Marie Wilson went to the Royal College of Music when she was fifteen, and three years later, while still a student, she became a member of the Queen's Hall Orchestra under the late Sir Henry Wood. This engagement was most welcome, not only because she had to help support her father, who was rapidly becoming a chronic invalid, but because few women had won places in the ranks of the leading professional orchestras in those days, and her achievement at such an early age was, to say the least, very encouraging. Thus, as a pupil of Maurice Sons (1857-1942, pupil of Wieniawski) at the College, and as a member of an orchestra under Sir Henry Wood's personal guidance, she received as good a musical education as any violinist in this country could desire.

In those days—the early nineteen-twenties—she also formed a string quartet which did particularly good work for the BBC during the first few years of broadcasting. Her time was then occupied with an amazingly full programme of concerts, recitals, broadcasts and recordings; so full, in fact, that in 1925 the demand for solo work had become so pressing that she was obliged to give up the Queen's Hall Orchestra.

The next four years saw her working chiefly as a soloist, and making an excellent reputation as such, but during 1929 the BBC approached her several times with a request that she should join the fine new symphony orchestra that the Corporation was about to assemble. She refused at least twice, but the temptation of a regular salary instead of the fluctuating income from solo work, and the news that some of the finest orchestral players in the world were entering this new orchestra eventually made her decide to accept the offer, and with some reluctance she gave up a substantial part of her solo work. She actually joined the BBC Symphony Orchestra in 1930, the year in which it was consolidated.

From being a rising young soloist, Marie Wilson became "without doubt the greatest woman orchestral player in the world". Those are Sir Adrian Boult's words, and are an apt tribute to this excellent violinist. After the resignation of the late Arthur Catterall (1883-1943) she became sub-leader to Paul Beard in the full ensemble, and leader of Section C.

To give an account of all the fine concerts, the wonderful tours and other experiences she enjoyed during those years as an orchestral player would take at least fifty pages, so little more can be said than a few passing words. Her popularity in the orchestra was no doubt due not only to her outstanding ability but to her sense of humour and "heartiness" generally. Everybody liked her. She took in good part, and even revelled in, the coarse little nickname (which shall not be repeated here) that referred to her enormous appetite! When the orchestra was on tour most of its members always upheld the musicians' tradition of washing down good music with good ale at a local tavern. Marie Wilson has never been very fond of strong drink, and would generally accompany them only if they could assure her that the "local" was one of those more hospitable places where "snacks at the counter" were available. Otherwise she would go off on her own, or with some other like-minded member, in search of a good restaurant . . . or two.

Another recognition of her achievements came in 1936 when she was made a professor at the Royal College of Music. She still holds this appointment, and takes the keenest interest in the various young students entrusted to her.

In October 1944 Marie Wilson left the BBC Symphony Orchestra in order to devote herself once again entirely to solo work. She did so not without regret, for her years in that ensemble had been very

happy ones, but it had become most difficult to fit in
her solo engagements with the orchestra's timetable, and
to have stayed with the BBC would probably have
meant spending the rest of her life as an orchestral
player. One of her first engagements after this decision
had been put into effect was to broadcast the Bax
violin concerto. Some idea of the impression she made
may be gained from a letter she received from the
composer himself a few days later. In this, Sir Arnold
says: "All my gratitude for your lovely performance
of my concerto last night. All your tempi are exactly
right—remarkably so. It was perfect, and I hope I
may hear you play it many times in future."

During the past three years or so, Marie Wilson
has built up an enviable reputation in concerto and
sonata work. She is essentially a classical violinist,
and readily acknowledges her allegiance to the "purist"
school of thought. She does not care for the "pretty"
style of playing. Her scholarly readings of Mozart
(especially the Concerto in A) and of the Beethoven
Concerto suggest that she has a deep feeling for the
works of these two composers. Her Bach, too, is
excellent, particularly in Concertos Nos. 1 in A minor,
2 in E, and 3 in D minor for two violins.

She takes a great interest in modern music, and her
repertoire includes concertos by Bloch, Bruch, Delius,
Vaughan Williams, Miaskovski and Prokofiev, as well
as the Bax Concerto. Mention might also be made
of the Brahms, Mendelssohn, Dvořák, Glazounov and
Saint-Saëns (No. 3) concertos, all of which appeal
strongly to her.

Marie Wilson's style is invariably good—sensitive
and assured—and she gets a very beautiful tone from
her Guadagnini. Her *cantabile* is always an outstanding
feature of her playing, due, no doubt, to her fine sense
of phrasing, a quality that is often insufficiently appreciated. She is one of those who prefer to keep to
the old-fashioned gut A string, but uses an aluminium-

covered D and the conventional silver-covered G. On the bow she uses all four fingers, lifting the little finger for *spiccato*, but does not believe that there need be any definite rule on the holding of the bow: it should be a matter of personal expedience. Of the eminent violinists she particularly admires, Ginette Neveu, Milstein and Heifetz are perhaps the most outstanding. Her experience of playing under eminent conductors has, of course, been extensive and beneficial, and she is especially grateful for the great work of the late Sir Henry Wood. Of the others, she esteems Sir Adrian Boult for his scholarship, Sir Malcolm Sargent for his vitality and love of hard work, Koussevitzky as a great trainer, and Toscanini for sheer genius. There are, of course, others for whom she has respect, but this is not the place for a critical survey of orchestral conductors.

Miss Wilson is very impressed by the amount of talent there is to-day among students of the violin: some of them seem to possess exceptional gifts as far as technique is concerned. This is not only in London: she was adjudicating at a festival in the provinces recently and found the same promise there. In spite of the pessimistic statements made from time to time by other prominent violinists, Miss Wilson feels that there are more opportunities for talented youth to-day than there were twenty or thirty years ago. Her chief concern is that although the general standard of playing is very high among students and amateurs, so many of them are guilty of lapses into bad intonation. She feels that this can best be remedied in the daily scale practice (she is a firm believer in regular daily practice) by *thoughtful* playing. It is useless to rip off scales without listening attentively to the sounds one produces.

To the young violinist she says: "Listen carefully to the playing of the great virtuosi, but do not copy the style of any one of them slavishly: it is better to take the best attributes of all and to mould your own style upon them.

Miss Wilson is a great believer in the "slow practice" method, and considers that sessions of an hour or an hour-and-a-half are quite long enough. Full-time students should arrange their work in sessions of this length and allow themselves to relax completely in the intervening periods. They should also remember the importance of maintaining a good physique: the performance of music is a most exacting and fatiguing occupation, and it cannot be done properly by those who feel tired most of the time. Late nights, if indulged in more than once or twice a week, can spoil the work of even the most gifted performer.

In her own career, she has found that her English name has been the greatest obstacle to popular success. English audiences are still influenced by foreign-sounding names, despite the fine achievements of British artists and composers during the past four or five decades.

Miss Wilson is absolutely free of affectation: she has no use whatever for musical snobbery. On two or three occasions she has taken part in light music performances, and quite enjoyed them. Some time ago she appeared in a variety programme at Douglas, Isle of Man, with Issy Bonn, and, incidentally, drew one of the greatest audiences she had ever known. She is a keen radio listener, enjoying not only the music but plays and such programmes as "Ignorance is Bliss" and "Merry-go-round". Dance music, if it is well played, always appeals to her, and she has a particular liking for rumbas if the rhythm is good. She can always enjoy an evening at the theatre or a good book by her fireside. Her literary taste is for such authors as Jane Austen, Dickens, Hugh Walpole and John Galsworthy, though you will also find a selection of thrillers stuffed in odd corners of her bookshelves.

But if she were asked what subject, apart from music, was foremost in her mind, she would reply promptly and candidly: "Food". It is a standing joke enjoyed by herself as much as by her friends. She believes wholeheartedly in the value of good, nourishing food prepared in an appetizing manner. In the kitchen she is quite a genius, in fact her friends declare that she could probably earn as much practising the culinary art in a West End restaurant as she can wielding the bow in the concert hall. Sooner or later one of our enterprising young composers will probably write a rhapsody about Marie Wilson's cakes.

EFREM ZIMBALIST

OUR last sketch is of a celebrated artist who in this country is rather less known to-day than most of the other world-famous violinists: Efrem Zimbalist.

He was born at Rostov-on-Don in April 1889, son of Alexander Zimbalist an orchestral conductor who gave him a good grounding in music. The first fourteen years of his life were more or less uneventful, though even as a boy he was such a reliable little violinist that at the age of nine he was allowed to lead the orchestra in the opera house at Rostov. In 1903 he entered the St. Petersburg Conservatoire and had the honour of studying under the great Leopold Auer. His studentship at this famous academy, in the company of many others who were later to rise to world-wide fame, was brilliant in every way, and nobody was surprised when he won the coveted gold medal and the Rubinstein scholarship of 1,200 roubles.

Most of his early triumphs took place beyond the borders of his native land. He made his first appearance in Germany at a Berlin concert on 7 November 1907 and gave a sensational rendering of the Brahms Concerto. Two months later he was in London, and it is interesting to turn back the pages of history, as it were, and see what the *Musical Times* had to say about his début here on 9 December. The following extract is from the January (1908) issue of that journal:

"A fellow student of Mischa Elman under Professor Auer, and styling himself 'Zimbalist', made his first appearance in London on December 9th at

Queen's Hall. The newcomer, stated to be only fourteen[1] years of age, possesses musical talent and executive facility extraordinary for his years, even in these days of youthful precocity. Supported by the London Symphony Orchestra, conducted by Mr. Landon Ronald, he played the solo part of Tchaikovsky's Violin Concerto with such firmness and brilliancy as to excite enthusiastic applause. He was heard to greater advantage, however, in Lalo's *Symphonie Espagnole*, a work that seemed to be more within the range of his expressive powers. That Zimbalist will become an artist of the first rank there can be little doubt."

After a prolonged tour of European countries that lasted nearly three years, Zimbalist made his début in America with the Boston Symphony Orchestra on 27 October 1911. His success was instantaneous : rarely had the Glazounov Concerto been played in such a rich, colourful manner. Everybody marvelled at his glorious tone, his exquisite *cantilena* and faultless technique, so it was not surprising that offers of other engagements were showered upon him for months afterwards.

During the next two or three decades he was to go to all corners of the earth. His concert tours have taken him well over a million miles—an average of more than 30,000 a year. Typical of the longer tours is the one he made some years ago when he went from America to Australia, then turned northwards and went right through Japan, returned to Australia by another route, and then did a seemingly endless tour of most of the European countries. He has made no less than six tours of the Far East, and in the days when the Emperor of Japan was regarded as a deity he was accorded the rare privilege of hearing the Imperial Orchestra. Only two or three other visitors from the Western Hemisphere had thus been honoured.

[1]This is incorrect of course.

Zimbalist's first marriage, which took place in London on 15 June 1914, was to Alma Gluck, the eminent soprano singer, who frequently toured with him. Shortly afterwards she gave up her career entirely to devote herself to her husband and home. They had two children: Maria (now Mrs. Henry F. Bennett, Jnr.) and Efrem.

After the death of Alma Gluck, Zimbalist married Mary Louise Curtis Bok in 1943. Mrs. Bok was the widow of Edward E. Bok, who won the Pulitzer Prize for his book *The Americanization of Edward Bok*. He founded the famous Curtis Institute of Music, Philadelphia, of which Zimbalist has been the Director since 1941, having joined its faculty in 1928.

The outstanding qualities of Zimbalist's playing are his superb, rich tone, which is astonishingly powerful at times yet never seems to be forced, and his incredible technique, which according to one critic is "as near perfect as any human violinist is likely to get." He plays with very great feeling, but always remains well poised and seems to keep surprisingly cool. He does not indulge in musical extravagance, and has no airs and graces.

Zimbalist has composed quite a lot of music, including songs and piano music as well as pieces for the violin. His orchestral compositions include a concert phantasy on Rimsky-Korsakov's *Coq d'or*; *American Rhapsody*; a tone poem entitled *Portrait of an Artist* which was first performed by the Philadelphia Orchestra on 7 December 1945; and a Concerto in C-sharp minor for violin and orchestra, first played in public on 28 November 1947, by the composer with the Philadelphia Orchestra under Eugene Ormandy. He has also written an effective Sonata in G minor for violin and piano, a String Quartet in E minor, and a suite of Spanish dances called *Sarasateana*.

He has always specialized in modern music, and many of our twentieth-century composers have reason to feel grateful to him for introducing their work to the public. A substantial part of his spare time is spent in examining new works of living composers, and few things give him more pleasure than to announce his discovery of a really promising work from some young composer who is struggling to achieve recognition. Among the many new works he has introduced are the concertos of Ernest Schelling, Frederick Stock, John Powell, Albert Spalding and Tor Aulin. During the 1947-8 season he gave an important series of historical violin recitals in New York City.

A genial personality, modest in the extreme, and a great wit, Zimbalist loves good company, and his friends say that he will throw a party at the slightest provocation. He enjoys good vintage wines and is a connoisseur of cigars, much to the delight of those who have the honour of joining him for an evening's chamber music, for he is always most generous, and consequently there is something of a fifty-thousand-a-year atmosphere about the place by the end of the evening. Such hospitality does not bear thinking about in this land of austerity. An evening with Zimbalist generally concludes with bridge or poker, but unless you are an exceptionally good player it is better to think of some ingenious excuse for an early departure.

During the greater part of his life Zimbalist has been an incorrigible collector. When on his world-wide tours he spent most of his spare time scouring old bookshops and antique dealers' showrooms, and had some remarkable "finds"—less in recent years, perhaps, owing to the growing astuteness of the gentlemen who run these establishments. His library of precious first editions and manuscripts became so large a few years ago that he was compelled to sell part of it by auction.

He also acquired one of the finest collections of violins in the world, but has now sold most of these historic instruments; one of the exceptions being his famous "Titian" Stradivarius, which some authorities consider to be the most lovely-toned fiddle in existence.

Another of his hobbies was the collecting of what he calls Orientalia, and for many years he specialized in ancient Japanese medicine cases and Chinese snuff bottles. Most forms of Eastern art appeal strongly to him, and any visitor to his home would discover specimens of such works that amply justify his enthusiasm for the art treasures of the Orient.